Roadfood Sandwiches

Roadfood Sandwiches

RECIPES AND LORE FROM OUR
FAVORITE SHOPS COAST TO COAST

JANE *and* MICHAEL STERN

 HOUGHTON MIFFLIN COMPANY * BOSTON NEW YORK 2007

For information about permission to reproduce
selections from this book, write to Permissions,
Houghton Mifflin Company, 215 Park Avenue South,
New York, New York 10003.

Visit our Web site: www.houghtonmifflinbooks.com.

Library of Congress Cataloging-in-Publication Data
Stern, Jane.
Roadfood sandwiches : recipes and lore from our
favorite shops coast to coast / Jane and Michael Stern.
p. cm.
Includes index.
ISBN-13: 978-0-618-72898-5
ISBN-10: 0-618-72898-8
1. Sandwiches. 2. Cookery, American. I. Stern,
Michael. II. Title.
TX818.S75 2007 641.8'4—dc22
2006030494

Book design by Lisa Diercks
The text of this book is set in Belizio.

Food styling by Mary Jane Sawyer
Prop styling by Colleen Gannon

Printed in the United States of America
MP 10 9 8 7 6 5 4 3 2 1

For our dear friend Elizabeth Nell,
who always knows when it's time to go

Acknowledgments

Thank-you #1 goes to Roger Waynick, whose inspiration was the genesis of this book. Roger sparkles with ideas, and it has been our good fortune to bask in that radiance.

Our agent, Doe Coover, kept the faith during this book's extra-long gestation, and our editor, Rux Martin, kept us on the beam even when we had lost track of where that beam was. Extra-special thanks are due to Frances Kennedy, without whose help nothing would have happened.

We especially want to thank the travel companions who go with us everywhere, at least in spirit, whenever we go looking for good things to eat: at *Gourmet* magazine, Ruth Reichl, James Rodewald, John (Doc) Willoughby, and Larry Karol; at Roadfood.com, Big Steve Rushmore and Stephen Rushmore, Jr., Kristin Little, Marc Bruno, Cindy Keuchle, and Bruce Bilmes and Sue Boyle; and at public radio's *The Splendid Table,* Sally Swift, Lynne Rosetto Kasper, and Jen Russell.

Finally, it should be apparent that we did not create this book out of whole cloth. We would have nothing if it were not for the cooks, chefs, waiters, proprietors, and their spouses who have created great restaurants and delicious sandwiches and who have shared the recipes and stories that go with them. It has been a pleasure to work with these people all around the country. To do justice to their achievements has been our guiding principle all along.

RECIPE NOTE: All recipes have been edited for consistency; those not specifically attributed to a chef or restaurant are the authors'.

Contents

ROADFOOD

viii

SANDWICHES

ROADFOOD

xiv

SANDWICHES

Roadfood
Sandwiches

Introduction

America is a wonderland of sandwiches. Every region, every city, every family, has its favorites, and it is rare indeed to find any two that are exactly alike. Some are austere, like the plain, perfect fried fish sandwich Coleman's sells in the old market of Wheeling, West Virginia; others are baroque, like the goopy, soupy hot brown of Louisville, Kentucky. There are rich ones served in tumbledown shacks: the crab roll at Red's Eats on the Maine shore. And there are plebeian ones made by cutting-edge chefs: liver 'n' onions with firecracker sauce at the Old Post Office on Edisto Island, South Carolina. Sandwiches with ethnic roots abound: Italian roast pork in Philadelphia, the ubiquitous diner souvlaki, the multiple-meats, high-protein Uruguayan chivito, Nebraska's Russian/German meal in a pastry known as a bierock. Many sandwiches are only-in-America delights: pimento cheese throughout the South, New Mexico's roast green chile wrap, New Orleans' oyster loaf, Great Lakes walleye (with beer on the side, of course).

You can travel coast to coast eating nothing but sandwiches, never having the same kind twice, and discover some of the most enjoyable one-of-a-kind restaurants along the way. This book's sandwich sources are as varied as the landscape, from the film noir sawdust floors of Philippe the Original in Los Angeles (home of the French dip) to the al fresco picnic tables of the Clam Box on Massachusetts' North Shore. A few of our favorite recipes come from quite civilized dining establishments: chicken Vesuvio at Harry Caray's in Chicago; sardines on rye at the Pine Club in Dayton, Ohio; spiedini of beef at Louie's Backyard in Key West. A lot hail from diners (Becky's of Portland, Maine), street carts (Roque's Carnitas of Santa Fe), butcher shops (In't Veld Meat Market of Pella, Iowa), and bars (McBob's of Milwaukee).

For so many Americans, sandwiches are a vital part of our culinary selves, an identity marker nearly as distinct as DNA. Tell us what you call a sandwich of warm roast beef with gravy, and we will tell you where you're from. If you call it Italian beef, you are from Chicago. If it's beef on weck, you are a Buffalonian. If you ask for it with debris (succulent scraps from the roasting pan or cutting board), you are from New Orleans. Call it wet beef or beef Manhattan, and we'd bet you live in Kansas or the western plains. Hot beef is strictly an Upper Midwest term. French dip used to be southern Californian but is now more generally western.

The tubular segment of bread that is sliced lengthwise and filled with cold cuts or hot meats has enough variations and aliases to make a book: hero and submarine throughout the East (except in Westchester County, New York, where—inexplicably—it is known as a wedge, and in much of Connecticut, where it's a grinder). It is nowhere more popular (or better) than in the Delaware River Valley, where the term "hoagie" supposedly began as "hoggie" because during World War I, Italian ship workers in Philadelphia's Hog Island became known for the gigantic sandwiches they brought for lunch. "Hoagie" usually is applied only to cold variations (although we've seen hot hoagies, too). Midwestern state fairs offer a hot or cold variation of the theme as an Italian sandwich, or by its politically incorrect name, Guinea sandwich. In Portland, Maine, the word "sandwich" is redundant. Step up to the counter and order an Italian.

Similarly, throughout Florida, as well as in New York City, the term "Cuban" refers not only to a person from Cuba or a Havana cigar, but also to a layered sandwich that contains two kinds of pork, white cheese, pickle, and mustard inside a tube of fluffy-centered Cuban bread. Louisiana Acadians call their multilevel variant a pirogue, after the old-time bayou canoe, and in New Orleans it is a po' boy, because back in 1929 the sandwiches were offered by French Quarter restaurateurs to striking streetcar workers, who were "poor boys."

Egalitarian-minded readers will notice that this book's contents are not equally balanced among states and regions. Rather than include two recipes from each of the fifty states, we have focused on what we know and love and can recommend wholeheartedly: the best sandwiches we have eaten in our travels around the country, as served at our favorite restaurants. It has long been our belief that a dish, or a sandwich, is far more interesting when you know who makes it, who invented it, who eats it, and where and how it's served.

You'll notice that there are no hamburgers, barbecue sandwiches, or hot dogs in this book. The omission is not because we disrespect them; on the contrary, each deserves a book of its own. The question is: are they sandwiches? They fit the most basic meaning of the term—ingredients enclosed by or supported by bread—but they are defined less by their sandwichness than by other, more important measures. Hamburgers are a matter of meat and condiments, and while the quality of the bun can surely make a huge difference, a great hamburger satisfies a different facet of human hunger from a great sandwich. The same goes for barbecue and hot dogs. To think of these three as sandwiches is like thinking of handguns, shotguns, and rifles as tools. Yes, they are, but if we were writing a book on the subject, we wouldn't think to include them along with hammers and saws.

Sandwiches are not uniquely American. Many of the world's fine cuisines have ways of neatly pocketing meat or vegetables inside breadstuffs (what would we moderns do without the Mideast's pita bread?). The sandwich as we know it was actually invented in England, when, two centuries ago, the fourth Earl of Sandwich ordered meat brought to him on bread so his meal wouldn't divert him from the gambling tables, but it's this country that's gone hog wild with the concept. Perhaps that's because sandwiches are, by their very nature, casual food. They are at home on a picnic table, perfect for snacks, easy to eat as well as to make at any time of day. What could be more truly, democratically American than a meal at which you don't have to worry about which fork to use or what wine to serve?

Sandwichcraft

Is there anyone who cannot make a sandwich? Most of us admit to at least a few self-doubts when we have to engage in serious cooking (mixing, souffléing, grilling, and the like), but when it comes to sandwiches, who does not consider himself or herself a master? We all have our own version of the classics—tuna, PB&J, BLT, and the ever-popular *what's-in-the-refrigerator?*-on-white. But there is more to sandwichery than these comfortable fundamentals. Sandwiches can be the world's easiest way to create novel meals without producing a lot of unwanted kitchen heat.

After all, the only things you need to construct a great one are some interesting ingredients and a condiment or two. If you've got the supplies, you can put a great sandwich together nearly as quickly as shuffling a deck of cards.

Here are a few basic guidelines for happier sandwich making and eating.

BREAD

The exoskeleton of a sandwich can be almost any kind of bread that doesn't crumble too easily. The importance of the bread ranges from a plain vehicle whose purpose is little more than transporting ingredients from plate to mouth—as in, say, a BLT—to the raison d'être for a sandwich in which the ingredients play second fiddle. A good example of the latter is the traditional Cuban morning bread: a toasted length of feather-light, crisp-crusted baguette spread merely with butter. Or a hot-from-the-oven salt bagel containing only cream cheese to cushion its saline punch.

There are four basic bread forms for sandwiches: the slice, the loaf, the wrap, and the roll, the last category including bagels, croissants, biscuits, and any other individually sized hunk of bread that can be sliced and stuffed. Local variations of rolls and names for them are near-infinite, including bulkies, kaisers, hard rolls, long rolls, and Ports (short for Portuguese rolls).

Sliced bread tends to make the most wieldy sandwiches, even for triple-deckers, because slices can be hoisted easily in one hand (or possibly two hands) and because their planar shape is generally good at containing all but the sloppiest ingredients. While crustless sandwiches are pretty, crust does serve a purpose, shoring in juicy things between the slices. As a rule, the thicker the sandwich, the more essential a sturdy crust.

Small loaves can be quite manageable, especially if they are not overstuffed and if the ingredients aren't really goopy, like an Italian Parmesan with lots of sauce. Some loaves are slightly scooped out—their soft centers removed—so the filling will fit better, which makes for a sandwich that is easy to pick up but still runs a high risk of disintegrating after a bite or two. The extreme example of this latter problem is the New Orleans oyster loaf, aka oyster boat, which tends to be more knife-and-fork fare than something you'd consider eating out of hand. Some New Orleans restaurants make their oyster boats not in tubular French breads but in whole, full-size sandwich loaves, one entire loaf per sandwich!

A great dilemma for many bread-loving sandwich makers who use loaves, rolls, or such Italian breads as ciabatta or focaccia is that the best of them are chewy and sturdy-crusted, meaning that the firm bite required almost inevitably causes malleable ingredients—like tuna salad, peanut butter, and soft cheese—to squish out. The only solutions are to make mini sandwiches, deconstruct the sandwich and eat the top and bottom halves separately, or live with the drippage.

Every bit as much as top-quality ingredients, good bread can make or break a sandwich. Corned beef on supermarket rye cannot hold a candle to the same corned beef on slick-crusted, chewy sourdough rye. Likewise, a Delaware Valley hoagie demands to be made on a rugged length of fresh-baked Italian bread, and no matter how good the beef is in Buffalo, it is not a real beef sandwich unless the roll is a genuine kummelweck spangled with coarse salt and caraway seeds.

CHEESE

Some cheese exists for sandwiches: Swiss, American, Muenster. And while provolone is fine when melted in a casserole, its true destiny is to be the rich, heat-softened blanket atop sauced meats in a hot Italian hero.

Modern sandwichcraft tends to include many cheeses not formerly found between sliced bread: disks of fresh mozzarella (known in all delis of the Northeast as *mutz*), wedges of runny Brie and triple crème, even such unwieldy crumblers as Maytag blue and Gorgonzola.

The most basic use of cheese in a sandwich is as a solo act. God bless grilled cheese, even when it doesn't include bacon or tomato, and even if the bread is supermarket white. The balance of silky melted cheese and a crisp griddle-cooked envelope of bread around it is fundamental. (But please, let's at least have pickles on the side!) Likewise, we salute a thick pile of thin-sliced Swiss on fresh, crusty rye (preferably with butter and mayo) as well as the ultra-kitsch but hard-to-resist standby of Velveeta on supersoft Wonder, adorned, of course, with Miracle Whip.

Who doesn't love the classic combos: ham and Swiss, salami and provolone, roast beef and American? But there's also great joy to be had in mix-'n'-matching cheeses: American *and* Swiss with liverwurst, or a tuna salad patty melt topped not with a usual cold-cut companion but with see-through tiles of heat-softened hard cheese such as Parmesan or Asiago.

Aside from taste, the primary issue to consider when choosing cheese for a sandwich is texture. A really rugged salami requires an equally substantial cheese, lest the meat's chewiness totally eclipse the velvet-soft character of, say, Cheez Whiz. On the other hand, the uniformity of Whiz, especially when melted, makes it a perfect foil for the tender shreds of griddled beef in a Philly cheesesteak.

OTHER INGREDIENTS

There are few sandwiches that don't benefit from a film of butter spread on the bread, not only because the flavor of butter is complementary to so many things, but also because the butter seals the bread and thus prevents moist ingredients from leaching into it and turning it soggy. Needless to say, softened butter is best for spreading, especially on soft slices, and it's important to spread it everywhere and all the way to the edges.

Consider flavored butter. Starting with slightly softened butter, you can add crushed garlic, a bit of anchovy paste, mustard, herbs, lemon juice, wasabi, or curry powder to fit the ingredients.

Lettuce, parsley, cilantro, and any other leafy things should be patted very dry after they are washed. Similarly, you can limit the sog factor of very juicy tomatoes by laying the slices on a paper towel before putting them into the sandwich.

LEFTOVERS AND LEFTOVER SANDWICHES

The best-known leftovers sandwich maker is cartoon character Dagwood Bumstead, whose culinary gift is heaping an impossibly high tower of disparate leftovers between slices of bread, usually straight from the refrigerator in the middle of the night. Dagwood's heroic heaps of cold cuts, chicken parts, and hunks of roast gained such pop-culture notoriety in the 1930s that the name "dagwood" has endured as a term for any sandwich that is based on a pile of seemingly incongruent ingredients.

For serious fans of gravy-drenched sandwiches, leftovers are the best part of Thanksgiving dinner: day-after hot turkey sandwiches. Slices and scraps of white and/or dark meat are warmed (preferably in a microwave oven, so they stay moist) and arrayed on a couple of pieces of good soft white bread. The bread is sided by a volcano-shaped mound of mashed potatoes, either left over and reheated with a few extra shots of warm milk and butter or freshly made, and the whole shebang is blanketed with hot gravy. Like the potatoes, the gravy can be from the day before or it can be freshly made, or, when time and energy are limited, it can be store-bought. If you have some cranberry sauce from the turkey-day feast, so much the better; its sweet tang and bright red color add zest to the plate of beige leftovers that many consider the ultimate comfort food. Needless to say, this is a sandwich that demands utensils.

The possibilities for using leftovers in sandwiches are only as limited as your imagination. The only thing you don't want between the bread is something with bones (although we've seen bone-in pork chop sandwiches that work). Of course, any carved hunk of meat is a natural, hot or cold: turkey, chicken, ham, beef, pork. Have a few deviled eggs left over from a party? Chop them fine and make egg salad sandwiches. Yesterday's roasted vegetables, layered with creamy cheese between sturdy tiles of peasant bread, are irresistible. We love thin slices of leftover meat loaf on whole wheat bread with ketchup, lettuce, and mayo.

Then there's the issue of leftover sandwiches. That is, sandwiches you've made that don't get eaten. Well, what's better than ham and Swiss refrigerated overnight, then dipped in egg and griddle-cooked in plenty of butter to become a breakfast sandwich?

TOASTING

If you like toasted sandwiches, a kitchen tool well worth having is a plancha, a sandwich press that toasts both sides and squeezes the sandwich together. It compresses the ingredients, not only making for a less messy sandwich but also creating a great harmony of multiple layers. If you don't have a plancha, the effect can be approximated by cooking the sandwich in a large frying pan while using a smaller one to weigh it down (and of course flipping the sandwich once).

SERVING

Cutting a sandwich in half is almost always a good idea for easy eating. When cutting one with ingredients that are likely to squish out, consider assembling it without the top layer of bread, cutting through the ingredients and the bottom layer, and then cutting the top slice before applying it. When cutting a fully assembled squishy sandwich, use a sharp serrated bread knife and steady the sandwich with the fingers of the hand that isn't doing the slicing.

Always have more napkins than you think you need. The messier the sandwich, the more important this principle.

SIDE DISHES

So as not to suffer the sight of a lonely sandwich on a plate, most people like some kind of accompaniment. Proper kosher-style restaurants serve large bowls of pickles and pickled tomatoes that customers can nab to accompany an overstuffed sandwich. We find that pickles are particularly welcome alongside anything made from brisket—corned beef, pastrami, or brisket itself—because their briny smack sings in fine harmony with meat that is luxurious (i.e., fatty) and their crispness is an ideal contrast to the tenderness of long-cooked brisket and the brawn of good rye.

Lunch counters frequently escort sandwiches with a pickle spear or two or a sheaf of pickle chips, from sour dill to sweet bread-and-butter. One of us Sterns, who never met a condiment he didn't like, believes no grilled cheese sandwich is complete without a significant pickle presence.

Mini servings of salad are another option to round out a sandwich plate, although they bring the process of eating into another dimension, requiring a utensil. Non-kosher-style deli counters frequently offer little cups of potato salad and macaroni salad, along with a plastic fork. These sweet, tender lagniappes are a good foil for meat with substance: roast beef, ham, salami.

Some hot sandwiches are well-rounded meals unto themselves, such as the Kentucky hot brown (page 120); others, such as hot beef (page 117) and hot pork (page 122), absolutely demand mashed potatoes and gravy. Sometimes French fried potatoes will work in this context, especially if they can stand up under a blanket of gravy.

When it comes to cold sandwiches, chips are always in good taste. As a general rule, potato chips work best with seafood or such lightweight meats as chicken and turkey. Despite the recent explosion in artisanal chips, or whatever the rosemary-and-olive-oil boutique ones are called, plain potato chips are generally best if what you're looking for is a bit of salty crunch to balance the sandwich. Deluxe, high-priced chips tend to hog the flavor spotlight.

Any sandwich with pepper's heat, whether in the meat itself or in the condiments applied, needs a chip with earthy character to help cushion the fire. Corn chips are wonderful on the side of Iowa loosemeats (page 137) and Clementine's Meaty Chili and Cheddar (page 140), and in fact they are an essential companion for any sandwich that includes chili meat.

MUSTARD MUSTER

The panoply of condiments available to sandwich makers is vast, and there is no shortage of opinions as to which ones are best on what. Mayonnaise fans debate Duke's brand vs. Hellmann's (called Best Foods on the West Coast), especially when mixing tuna salad — not to mention the fundamental controversy of mayo vs. Miracle Whip. Ketchup's multiple personalities include jalapeño-spiked and green-tinted, and more exotic choices for dressing up a sandwich include hot pepper sauce, horseradish, and herbal jelly.

Of all the things that add pow to a sandwich, none is so provocative as mustard. Any ordinary grocery store has several dozen kinds from which to choose, and a good gourmet specialty store might have a hundred.

Here are the basic categories of mustard, within which you'll find all sorts of flavorings, consistencies, and mix-ins.

DIJON MUSTARD. True Dijon mustard must be made only from black mustard seeds mixed with either white wine, unripened grape juice, or vinegar. French law prohibits any mustard with sugar, flour, coloring, flavoring, or other additive to be called "Dijon." Dijon mustard is sinus-clearing sharp but not so hot that it burns the tongue.

GERMAN MUSTARD. Available either sweet or spicy, German mustard goes great with garlicky salami or any sort of sausage. As part of a Reuben sandwich with spicy corned beef, nothing's better.

GRAINY MUSTARD. A mustard appreciated for its rugged texture owing to the inclusion of bits of mustard seed. Beige in color, it tends to be relatively mild. While frequently served on the side of a hot meal (sausages, stout meats), it is an admirable cold-cut companion, too.

HONEY MUSTARD. Honey mustard has skyrocketed in popularity in the past decade. At its best, it is a tongue-teasing balancing act of sweet and hot that is especially welcome with sandwiches that contain pork or ham.

YELLOW MUSTARD. Also known as American mustard because it is the traditional condiment for hot dogs and deli sandwiches, yellow mustard has a silky consistency and is always bright yellow.

Amighetti Special

AMIGHETTI'S ✳ ST. LOUIS, MISSOURI

We could easily have written a book called *America's Best Hero Sandwiches*. One of the greats, and an essential St. Louis dish, is the Amighetti Special, as dished out at Amighetti's, a landmark sandwich shop on the Hill, which is the city's old Italian neighborhood.

Amighetti's is so casual that quality of service is not an issue. Place your order at the window and wait for your name to be called. Sandwiches are presented wrapped in butcher paper inscribed with the house motto: "Often Imitated, Never Duplicated." Take your sandwich to a seat, preferably in the sunny al fresco courtyard, unwrap, and feast. Afterwards, gelato is available to refresh the palate.

The full and formal name of this happy place is Amighetti's Café and Bakery, which gives you a clue to one reason that the sandwiches are so good: the place bakes its own bread. It is always impeccably fresh, sometimes still warm, and thick-crusted, with sturdy insides that beg to be loaded with cold cuts and cheeses galore.

Specialties include the Little Italy combo of salami, cheese, olives, onions, and garlic butter, as well as a three-cheese veggie sandwich for meat frowners. The top of the line is the Amighetti Special, which is ham, roast beef, salami, a few slices of cheese, a spill of hot pepperoncinis, and—the kicker—Amighetti's tangy-sweet house dressing.

The dressing is great on almost any hearty cold-cut sandwich and can be refrigerated for several days (although it loses its punch over time). We believe our recipe pretty well duplicates Amighetti's proprietary one.

3-4 tablespoons Special Sauce (recipe follows)
1 12-inch length of sturdy Italian bread, sliced in half lengthwise
3 slices ham
3 slices roast beef
4 slices Genoa salami
3 slices brick cheese
Lettuce
Tomato
Dill pickle slices
Sliced sweet onion
3-4 whole pepperoncini

Spread the special sauce on the cut sides of the bread. Layer all the ingredients on the bottom half of the bread. Top with the remaining bread and gently press.

Special Sauce

MAKES ABOUT 1 CUP (ENOUGH FOR FOUR 12-INCH HEROES)

½ cup mayonnaise
3 tablespoons sour cream
2 tablespoons prepared hot mustard
1 tablespoon prepared horseradish
1 tablespoon finely minced scallion
1 tablespoon chopped fresh dill

Combine all the ingredients in a small bowl and mix well.

Bacon and Egg on a Long Roll

TONY'S ✳ NEW YORK, NEW YORK

Breakfast sandwiches are ubiquitous, and it's rare to find one that's really bad. Some of the best breakfast sandwiches you will eat anywhere are in New York, at a street cart called Tony's, which parks at Nassau and Wall starting about 4 A.M., Monday through Friday. "Bread or platter?" asks Theodora Psaroudis, Tony's wife, when we order bacon and eggs.

"Platter," we say, assuming it the more comely choice.

"Wrong!" declares the man in line behind us, whose smock identifies him as a floor trader at the NYSE around the corner. "Bread's the best," he says. "Get a long roll."

Tony's fast food is not instantaneous. Eggs are cracked for every order, and there isn't room on the small griddle for more than a few at a time. During the five-minute wait, we ask the people at the juice cart next door to whip us up a mango-banana-orange-pineapple shake; the cup, its lid heaped with chunks of fresh fruit, comes in a brown paper bag. We pay Theodora $2.25 for a magnificent lode of buttery eggs and sizzled bacon folded inside a muscular hero roll with a silky seeded crust. The bread is especially delicious when imprinted with the eggs' butter and the bacon's drippings.

There is a difference between this sandwich and a bacon and egg on a hard roll, and it isn't only a difference in size. In addition to being larger, this style of breakfast sandwich is chewier. A hard roll can be relatively fluffy, but the nature of a New York–style long-roll sandwich depends on a tubular length of bread that has real muscle—less a matter of crust than of chew. That kind of character is needed to absorb all the juiciness of this luscious breakfast.

Be sure to cook the eggs in plenty of butter. It's the combo of bacon grease and butter that is this sandwich's flavor magic.

Cheese can be added simply by laying a slice or two (American cheese, please) on the bread before adding the eggs. The eggs' heat should be enough to soften and semimelt the cheese.

  4   strips medium-thick bacon
  2   tablespoons butter
  2   large eggs
  1   sturdy long roll (about 8 inches), sliced in half lengthwise (see headnote)

Cook the bacon in a large skillet on medium-high heat, turning it once, until it is not quite crisp. You want strips that are still fairly flexible. As the bacon cooks, melt the butter in another skillet and crack the eggs into the skillet. Fry the eggs sunny-side up, over easy, or over hard, as you prefer.

Use a spatula to lift the eggs from the skillet, scooping up as much melted butter as possible, and lay them inside the roll. Similarly, lift the bacon with a spatula and, without draining the strips, lay them on top of the eggs. Serve hot.

Baked Beans on Brown Bread

CAMBRIDGE, MASSACHUSETTS

The great chef Julia Child once confided to us that one of her favorite when-nobody's-looking snacks was baked beans on brown bread. This makes perfect sense for a longtime resident of Cambridge, Massachusetts (although she was born in Pasadena, California), because both baked beans and brown bread are Yankee to the core, as is the idea of making today's breakfast or lunch from yesterday's supper. The result is one of the best "leftover" sandwiches there is.

It isn't every day of the week you pile baked beans on brown bread. In the Boston area, it is mostly a Sunday ritual, probably going back to Pilgrim times, when cooking on the Sabbath was forbidden. The bread was steamed and the beans were baked on Saturday, and as both keep very well, it was only logical to combine them on Sunday morning. For those who don't mind cooking on Sunday, these sweet sandwiches make a great companion for a big, hearty bacon-and-egg breakfast.

It is entirely possible to make baked beans on brown bread from all store-bought ingredients. The process is hardly more complicated than warming up a loaf of brown bread and opening a can of beans. Needless to say, it is infinitely better if you make the bread and beans yourself. We won't provide a baked bean recipe here (assuming that everybody has a favorite), but we shall give you a first-class recipe for brown bread, based on one we used in *The Durgin-Park Cookbook*. (Durgin-Park opened in 1827 in Boston's Faneuil Hall, and its meals have defined New England cookery for generations.) This brown bread is good not only for baked bean sandwiches but also for all sorts of teatime sandwiches, spread with butter, cream cheese, or best of all, cream cheese and chopped walnuts.

12   slices Brown Bread (recipe follows)
3   tablespoons cream cheese, softened
2   cups baked beans, drained of excess liquid
1-2   tablespoons milk, if needed

Spread 6 slices of the brown bread with ½ tablespoon cream cheese each. Use a fork to coarsely mash the baked beans, adding a bit of milk if needed to make the rugged mash spreadable. Spread the baked beans on the other 6 slices of bread. Gently press the cream-cheese and baked-bean slices together and serve.

Brown Bread

MAKES 1 LOAF (12 SLICES)

⅓   cup whole wheat flour
⅓   cup all-purpose flour
⅓   cup yellow cornmeal
⅓   cup unseasoned dried bread crumbs
1   teaspoon baking soda
½   teaspoon salt
1   cup buttermilk
½   cup dark molasses
⅓   cup dark raisins

Mix the flours, cornmeal, bread crumbs, baking soda, and salt in a medium bowl. Stir in the buttermilk and molasses; do not overmix. Stir in the raisins.

Coat a 1½-quart metal steaming mold or a 1-pound coffee can with vegetable oil cooking spray. Pour in the batter, run a knife or spatula through the batter to remove any air pockets, and cover tightly with a lid or heavy-duty foil. Place the mold on a rack (if you don't have a rack, canning jar rings work very well) in a deep pot with a tight-fitting lid. Add enough hot water to reach two thirds up the sides of the mold; cover.

Bring the water to a boil. Then reduce the heat to a simmer and steam the bread for 2¼ hours. Check the pot from time to time to make sure the water is not boiling away. Remove the mold from the water and allow it to stand for 20 minutes; then turn the bread out onto a rack to cool. To serve, cut into slices.

✳✳ Beef on Weck

CHARLIE THE BUTCHER'S KITCHEN ✳✳ BUFFALO, NEW YORK

"Beef on weck" is Buffalo shorthand for "beef on kummelweck," the German word for a roll spangled with caraway seeds. The bread is shaped like a kaiser roll but crowned with a mantle of seeds and coarse salt so abundant that it crunches audibly when bitten. It is tawny, with an extraordinarily fine crumb. The roll's light texture is crucial because it is designed to cushion but not compete with the gentle feel of the sliced beef it encloses. The top half of a beef on weck roll is customarily immersed in the pan juices just long enough for it to start to soften before it is set atop the sandwich.

One of the best places to eat one is Charlie the Butcher's Kitchen, located in a former hot dog stand. It really is an open kitchen, surrounded by a low counter with stools and oilcloth-covered tables. It sports such homespun touches as an old porcelain stove and shelves of well-thumbed cookbooks. As in any good kitchen, the aromas are splendrous: warm beef and its savory juice, grilling sausages and locally made hot dogs, smoked ham (on Monday), meat loaf and gravy (on Tuesday).

Charlie Roesch's fans consider him the ultimate authority on meat of all kinds. Although he is a young man and has operated this restaurant only since 1993—a nanosecond compared to the century-and-a-half dynasty of Schwabl's (page 161)—he is hardly a Johnny-come-lately in the Buffalo beef scene. His father was a butcher, as was his grandfather (their slogan: "You know it's fresh if it comes from Roesch"). To honor the family trade, he wears a white hard hat on his head and a butcher's smock over his shirt and necktie as he works at the counters in the center of his restaurant, stirring soups, cutting cabbages for the Wednesday corned beef dinner, and slicing roasts for his own distinctive version of the city's signature sandwich.

As Mr. Roesch stood at his butcher block, rhapsodizing about his favorite subject—the cuisine of western New York—a loyal patron waiting at the order window offered support. "If Charlie the Butcher says it's so, it's so!" he declared, before ordering a beef on weck with a smoked Polish sausage on the side.

Charlie prepares his beef in a high-tech "cook and hold" oven that has an effect on meat that's similar to dry-aging. Roasts are loaded in at 5 P.M. and are ready to serve the next day for lunch, resulting in meat that is ridiculously tender. Of course it is sliced by hand on the butcher counter at the front of the restaurant. "To have your meat carved by a real butcher is special," Charlie says. "Some people come in here who have never seen that."

Charlie's method of preparing beef for wecks is to start with a 40-pound roast. Our recipe is more suited for a home cook.

Serve these with beer.

MAKES 8 TO 12 SANDWICHES

4	pounds Roast Beef, sliced (recipe follows)
8-12	Kummelweck Rolls (recipe follows)
	Horseradish or mustard (optional)

Slice the warm beef as thin as your knife can carve (do not do this in advance).

Slice a roll in half horizontally and dip the cut side of the top half briefly in the jus mixture, just long enough to moisten it. Pile about an inch of sliced beef on each bottom half (6 to 8 ounces per sandwich). Add horseradish and/or mustard if desired. Cap with the top half of the roll.

(An alternative preparation is to double-dip the weck, which means to dip both the top and bottom halves of the roll in the jus. This results in a sandwich that is so moist that a knife and fork may be necessary to eat it.)

ᐧ Roast Beef

An eye of round works fine in this recipe, but if you want to splurge, nothing makes better beef for sandwiches than a tenderloin. The latter is so lean that it benefits from a layer of fat (bacon, for instance) added to the top as it roasts. Whatever kind of roast you use, you'll need a meat thermometer.

MAKES ENOUGH FOR 8 OVERSTUFFED SANDWICHES OR 12 STINGY ONES

1	4- to 6-pound eye of round or tenderloin roast, at room temperature
3-4	strips bacon, if using tenderloin
	Salt and freshly ground pepper

Preheat the oven to 450 degrees.

Place the roast on a shallow rack in a roasting pan (fat side up if using a round roast, or topped with bacon if using a tenderloin). Sprinkle generously with salt and pepper. Add about ¼ inch of water to the bottom of the pan. Put the roast in the oven and immediately lower the temperature to 350 degrees. Cook until a meat thermometer inserted into the center of the roast reads 130 degrees for rare, the traditional temperature for beef on weck sandwiches. The cooking time will vary depending on the thickness of the roast, anywhere from 10 to 20 minutes per pound.

Remove the roast from the oven and let it sit, covered loosely with foil, for 10 to 15 minutes before slicing. Expect the internal temperature to rise about 5 degrees as the roast rests.

Pour the juice from the bottom of the roasting pan into a smaller pan or a large Pyrex measuring cup. Add enough water so the mixture is about one third natural juice and two thirds water. This will be the jus for the sandwich. Under no circumstances should you thicken this gravy.

✶✶ Kummelweck Rolls

- ¼ cup coarse salt
- ¼ cup whole caraway seeds
- ³/₄ teaspoon cornstarch, dissolved in 2 tablespoons warm water
- ¼ cup boiling water
- 12 hard rolls or kaiser rolls

Combine the salt and caraway seeds in a small bowl. Put the cornstarch mixture in a small saucepan, then stir in the boiling water. Return the mixture to a boil and cook, stirring, over medium-high heat for about 5 minutes, until it is thick enough to coat a spoon. Remove from the heat and let cool.

Preheat the oven to 350 degrees.

Place the rolls on a baking sheet. Brush the top of each roll with the cornstarch solution and then sprinkle them with the salt-caraway mixture. Bake for 4 to 5 minutes, or until the tops of the rolls are dry.

(While traditionally used for beef sandwiches, wecks are also wonderful for roast pork.)

✳ Benedictine and Bacon

LILLY'S ✳ LOUISVILLE, KENTUCKY

Many cities can't claim to have invented a single sandwich. Louisville is home to two (not to mention such other gastronomic triumphs as the mint julep, the old-fashioned cocktail, and Derby pie). While the hot brown (page 120) is recognized throughout the state and beyond, few people outside of Jefferson County have encountered the strange edible thing known as Benedictine cheese, which is the basis of this at once ladylike and hearty sandwich.

The ingredients of Benedictine cheese are innocuous . . . except for the essential green food coloring that can make it look like something from the table of the family Frankenstein. While our recipe calls for a couple of drops to create a graceful pastel, we have known Benedictineophiles from the punk school of cookery who would happily double that, all the better to give it the ghastly unnatural character they feel is its spiritual essence.

The cheese is a Victorian concoction named for its inventor, Jennie Benedict, a Louisville native who studied with Fannie Farmer in Boston and helped start the Louisville Business Women's Club in 1897. The dynamo known as Miss Jennie opened a tea room and soda fountain and was an immensely successful caterer as well as a beloved community volunteer (serving at the King's Daughters' Home for Incurables). She died in 1928, but her creation became essential in the repertoire of hostesses, and not only in the mid-South.

"How I love to give parties!" proclaimed the coloratura soprano Lily Pons in a 1942 issue of *American Cookery* that told of her cunning entertaining idea: parties with color themes. Her favorite was a pink party, where all the food was pink, from grenadine-laced gin to quivering crab apple salad to pink-frosted Lady Baltimore cake. For a woman who didn't want to be so rigorous of tint, how delightful it would be to use Benedictine cheese to construct a pink-frosted surprise sandwich layer loaf!

While still popular in many homes, Benedictine cheese rarely appears in any form on restaurant menus. But at Louisville's estimable Lilly's, where menus are imprinted with the hallelujah "God Bless Our Farmers" and where so much of the inventive, impromptu menu is devoted to the culinary heritage of the South in general and of Kentucky in particular, you'll find a beauty of a Benedictine and bacon sandwich. Follow that with dessert of banana bread pudding à-la-moded with roasted banana ice cream and wallowing in Myers's dark rum sauce, and we guarantee you will walk out humming "My Old Kentucky Home."

MAKES 3 SANDWICHES

½	cucumber, peeled, grated, and drained of moisture
1	bunch scallions, white parts and an inch or two of the green parts, finely chopped
8	ounces cream cheese, softened
1	tablespoon mayonnaise
1-2	drops green food coloring
6	slices whole wheat bread, crusts removed or not
9	strips bacon, cooked (not too crisp)
3	lettuce leaves

Mix the cucumber, scallions, cream cheese, and mayonnaise in a medium bowl. Add green food coloring by the drop, mixing each time to gauge the color. Spread one third of the mixture on each of 3 slices of the bread. Top the cream cheese with 3 slices of bacon, and top the bacon with the lettuce. So as not to squish the cheese too much when slicing, cut the sandwiches in half diagonally. Slice the remaining 3 slices of bread diagonally, place them on top, and serve.

✳ Bierock

The bierock goes back generations to the Volga Germans who settled on the American plains about a century ago. A hundred years earlier, they had left Germany for Russia to avoid religious persecution, but Russia turned out to be hostile too. During World War I and the Bolshevik revolution, many came to the fertile heartland of the United States and Canada. They brought with them their recipes for a baked yeast-dough bread pocket filled with beef, cabbage or sauerkraut, and onions. These portable meals (similar to the Upper Midwest's pasties, page 165) were a favorite lunch among farmworkers, and today they are ubiquitous at church suppers and fund-raisers throughout Nebraska and Kansas.

Descendants of the settlers knew bierocks also as runzies. Think of "bierock" as a cognate of "pierogi" or "burek"; the origins of the word "runza" are unknown. In 1949, Sally Everett and her brother, Alex Brening, opened the first Runza Drive-In in Lincoln, Nebraska. There are now more than sixty Runza locations in the region, and this is one of the few restaurant chains that an adventurous traveler ought to visit. The unusual sandwich they sell, trademarked as a Runza, long predates the first official Runza Drive-In.

Serve the sandwiches with pickles on the side.

MAKES 6 BIEROCKS

DOUGH

2	packages active dry yeast
1	cup sugar
³/₄	cup water, at room temperature
4-5	cups all-purpose flour
2	teaspoons salt
³/₄	cup milk, lukewarm
½	cup shortening
2	large eggs

FILLING

- 4 tablespoons (½ stick) butter
- ¾ cup chopped onion
- 1½ cups chopped cabbage
- ½ pound ground chuck
- 1 teaspoon salt
- ¼ teaspoon freshly ground pepper

PREPARE THE DOUGH: Combine the yeast, 1 tablespoon of the sugar, and ¼ cup of the water in a small bowl. Set aside for 5 minutes, until it begins to foam.

Combine 4 cups of the flour with the salt in a large bowl. Stir in the yeast mixture. Stir in the remaining sugar, remaining ½ cup water, and the milk, shortening, and eggs. Mix well. Turn out on a floured board and knead for 5 minutes, adding flour as necessary to create a smooth dough. Return the dough to the cleaned bowl, cover the bowl with plastic wrap or a damp towel, and set it aside in a warm, draft-free place while you prepare the filling. Let it rise to nearly double in size, about 45 minutes.

PREPARE THE FILLING: Melt the butter in a large skillet. Add the onion and cabbage and sauté over medium-low heat, stirring, until they are soft. Add the beef and cook until it is browned. Add the salt and pepper. Remove from the heat.

MAKE THE BIEROCKS: Lightly spray a baking sheet with vegetable oil cooking spray. With a rolling pin, roll out the dough into a 12-x-18-inch rectangle and cut it into 6 squares, about 6 inches across. Place a scant ¼ cup of the filling onto the center of each square and fold up the corners of the square, pinching the dough together to seal in the mixture. Place the stuffed squares seam side down on the baking sheet. Cover loosely with a clean kitchen towel and let them rise in a warm place for 45 minutes.

Preheat the oven to 375 degrees.

Bake the bierocks for 20 to 25 minutes, until golden brown. Serve warm.

✳ BLT Without Meat

Claire's Corner Copia is not just a place to eat. It is a lifestyle and a landmark. Opened in 1975 across the street from the Old Campus at Yale University, it is one of America's oldest and best-loved vegetarian restaurants. In addition to serving food, it serves as a gallery for local artists, sponsors classes in cooking and healthy eating, and has supported good community causes of all kinds.

Since its inception, Claire's has developed a vast library of winning recipes. We guarantee that no home cooks would complain if we included a few dozen of the restaurant's great sandwiches in this book, for the variety and color of the dishes served here are nothing short of spectacular. In fact, Chef Claire Criscuolo has written three excellent cookbooks: *Claire's Corner Copia Cookbook, Claire's Italian Feast,* and *Claire's Classic American Vegetarian Cooking.*

When we asked our old friend for some of her favorite sandwich recipes, she sent them to us with a signature that identified her as Chef Claire Criscuolo, R.N.

"R.N.?" we asked.

Claire explained: "The R.N. is for 'registered nurse,' something I practiced in my past life. Frank [Claire's husband] thought I should not let people know about my being a nurse until after I established myself as a chef so as not to scare off those people who back then thought healthy food meant awful-tasting foods. I have always believed that my profession as chef, every bit as much as registered nurse, is about preventing illness through delicious foods."

With that, she presented us with a recipe for the healthiest BLT we've ever sunk our teeth into. Not only is it strictly vegetarian, but Claire gives it a unique Italian flavor by including arugula and balsamic vinegar and by making it on Italian bread.

The brands Claire recommends are Spectrum Organic for dairy-free vegan mayonnaise and Lightlife Smart Bacon for the soy bacon.

¼ cup mayonnaise or organic dairy-free vegan mayonnaise

10 large leaves fresh basil, finely chopped

8 strips soy bacon

1 bunch (about 4 ounces) organic arugula, trimmed of tough stems

1 large tomato, heirloom if available, cut into bite-size cubes

2 teaspoons extra-virgin olive oil

2 teaspoons balsamic vinegar

 Salt and freshly ground pepper to taste

1 loaf whole wheat Italian bread, sliced in half lengthwise and then crosswise into four 3-inch-wide pieces, or 4 whole wheat buns

Stir together the mayonnaise and basil in a cup.

Heat a large skillet over medium-high heat. Spray the skillet with sunflower-oil or olive-oil cooking spray. Arrange the soy bacon strips in a single layer in the skillet. Cook for 2 to 3 minutes per side, or until the bacon reaches a medium brown color.

Place the arugula and tomato in a bowl. Drizzle the oil evenly over the top, and then, using tongs or two spoons, toss to coat. Drizzle the vinegar evenly over the arugula and tomato and sprinkle with salt and pepper. Toss well to combine. Taste for seasonings.

Cut each bun, if using, in half horizontally. Cut each strip of soy bacon in half.

To assemble the sandwiches, spread the bottom half of each sandwich piece or bun with 1 tablespoon of the basil mayonnaise, then top with 4 strips bacon and one fourth of the arugula-tomato mixture. Cover the sandwich with the top half of the bread or bun and serve.

✳✳ Breaded Steak

The breaded steak sandwich is unique to the South Side of Chicago around the old stockyards neighborhood, which gained infamy first in Upton Sinclair's *The Jungle* and later as the home of the Mayors Daley. A few years ago we went on an expedition to this part of town, known as Bridgeport, to compare and contrast different breaded steak sandwiches. But we found too few contenders for a serious taste-off. The only ones worth the trip were at Ricobene's on 26th Street (where some say the idea originated) and at Freddie's on 31st. (We have since heard that Kansas City has a very similar sandwich. Could it be a meatpacker's thing?)

Curiously, both restaurants are probably more widely known for their Italian beef (page 126) and their pizza, and Ricobene's French fries are among the city's elite. But to diehard lovers of old Chicago South Side cuisine, it's the breaded steak that inspires pilgrimages.

Of all the messy sandwiches that can be picked up in two hands, this may be the messiest, and it therefore requires a very rugged length of bread. Gonnella brand is a big favorite for fall-apart sandwiches throughout the city. Ricobene's boasts that it uses Turano French bread, which is more muscular than any other French bread we have ever met.

International cooks will note that the steak itself is something like a Milanese, which is a bread-crumb-crusted veal cutlet fried to a crisp. But by the time this sandwich is constructed and smothered with marinara sauce—known as gravy—all resemblance to the fine *cotolette alla Milanese* is lost.

MAKES 1 SANDWICH

All-purpose flour
1   8- to 10-ounce flank steak
1   large egg
1   tablespoon water
½   cup seasoned dried bread crumbs
1   tablespoon grated Parmesan cheese
¼   teaspoon salt
¼   teaspoon freshly ground pepper
    Vegetable oil for deep-frying
1   10- to 12-inch length sturdy Italian bread, sliced open horizontally
    (do not cut in half)
¼   cup shredded mozzarella cheese (optional)
⅓   cup marinara sauce, warmed
    Jarred bell peppers, giardiniera, or hot peppers to taste
    Roasted red bell peppers (see page 89)

Sprinkle a bit of flour on a smooth, clean surface. Flip the steak on the flour a couple of times so it has some flour on both sides and then use a meat pounder to pound it to less than ¼ inch thick and nearly a foot square. Mix together the egg and water in a wide, shallow dish. In a separate wide, shallow dish, combine the bread crumbs, Parmesan, salt, and pepper. Pour 3 inches of oil into a large skillet and heat it to 360 degrees. Dip the steak into the egg mixture, turning and folding until it is fully moistened. Then dredge it in the breadcrumb mixture, turning to coat it thoroughly. Slide the steak into the hot oil and cook until it is light brown, turning it once, about 4 minutes; do not let the steak brown too much.

Remove the steak from the pan, place it on paper towels, and instantly roll it up so it will fit inside the bread. Immediately place it in the loaf and top it with the mozzarella, if using. Pour on the marinara and add the condiments as desired. Don't be concerned if you are now staring at a plate of food that scarcely bears any resemblance to a portable sandwich. This is the way a breaded steak should look.

Buffalo Chicken

CARMINUCCIO'S ✳ NEWTOWN, CONNECTICUT

We cannot tell a lie: the foremost thing to eat at Carminuccio's is not a sandwich but pizza. Here is some of the most delicious pizza in Connecticut—no slight praise, given the fact that Connecticut is the home of the best pizza on earth. Our favorite toppings are roasted garlic and red peppers, but even plain cheese is superb on these thin, crisp Neapolitan-style crusts. Also outstanding are Carminuccio's stuffed breads: whole loaves packed with loads of such succulent combos as sausage and broccoli or capicola and provolone.

Nothing about the menu is outlandish or surprising. The excellence of this inconspicuous place along Route 25 has more to do with the high quality of the ingredients and the expert way in which they are assembled . . . which brings us to the subject of sandwiches. It's almost a shame the pizzas are so good, because many people get hooked on them and never take the opportunity to plow into Carminuccio's cornucopian Italian special or exemplary cheesesteak, or the zesty beauty known as a Buffalo chicken wing grinder.

In fact, there are no wings at all in this sandwich, but the wing formula, as perfected by Teresa Bellissimo of the Anchor Bar in Buffalo, New York, is its inspiration. The essentials of the dish are chicken meat—in this case, chicken breast meat—that is sopped with lip-tingling barbecue sauce combined with cool, creamy blue cheese dressing. Carminuccio's offers the sandwich two different ways: with slices of grilled chicken or slices of fried chicken. While the fried chicken version is actually closer to the traditional Buffalo wings, we like it with grilled chicken. It's practically health food!

MAKES 1 SANDWICH

8 thin slices grilled chicken breast (about 3 ounces)
2 tablespoons of your favorite barbecue sauce (hot and vinegary is customary)
1 6-inch grinder roll
3 slices American cheese
   Shredded lettuce
   Sliced tomato
   Salt and freshly ground pepper to taste
2 tablespoons blue cheese dressing (store-bought is fine)

In a medium skillet, sauté the grilled chicken in the barbecue sauce for 2 minutes to heat it through.

Slice the roll lengthwise and toast the inside lightly. Immediately lay the slices of American cheese over the bottom half of the roll so the heat softens them. Place the warm chicken and sauce on top of the cheese. Top the chicken with lettuce, tomato, salt and pepper, and finally with the blue cheese dressing. Close the sandwich and serve hot.

✱✳ Cajun Ham Po' Boy

While Austin, Texas, isn't exactly Louisiana, Hoover Alexander explains the excellent Cajun flavors featured in his restaurant by noting, "We're perched in the middle of the continent and our food reflects it. Down-home, comfort, soul, Tex-Mex, southwestern, Caribbean, BBQ, Cajun, Creole, Deep South, Gulf Coast seafood—the mix of the food on our tables is a mirror image of the geographical, racial, and ethnic boiling pot that makes Texas the great place it is." Of all those influences, Cajun is one of the strongest. Daily specials at the restaurant include the traditional red beans and rice every Monday, smoked boudin sausage on Friday, and Cajun pork roast or crawfish étouffée on Sunday.

While Mr. Alexander is himself a native Texan, he honed his Cajun-cooking chops back in the 1980s at a New Orleans–themed restaurant in Austin called Toulouse. It was there he developed a citywide reputation as a great Cajun cook. In 1998 he partnered up with local restaurateur Vernon O'Rourke to open Hoover's Cooking. Since then, it has become Austin's definitive down-home place to eat.

Hoover's Cooking makes its own Cajun seasoning to spice up the ham that is the main ingredient in this classic po' boy combo, but Mr. Alexander assures us that good store-bought Cajun seasoning will do the trick.

MAKES 1 PO' BOY

LETTUCE DRESSING

- ½ cup mayonnaise
- 1 tablespoon spicy mustard of choice
- ½ teaspoon Tabasco sauce
- ½ teaspoon minced fresh garlic
- 2-3 cups shredded iceberg lettuce, chilled

SANDWICH

- 1 hoagie roll

  Butter
- 4 ounces shaved smoked ham (a 1-inch pile)

  Cajun seasoning to taste
- 2 slices Swiss cheese

  Chopped tomato

Preheat a cast-iron grill pan or the broiler.

PREPARE THE DRESSING: Stir together the mayonnaise, mustard, Tabasco, and garlic in a medium bowl. Stir in the lettuce.

ASSEMBLE THE SANDWICH: Slice the hoagie roll in half lengthwise, butter the inside, and toast the inside in the grill pan or under the broiler until light brown. Set the roll aside.

Dust the ham with Cajun seasoning and grill or broil it until hot. Lay the hot ham on the bottom half of the hoagie roll and immediately top it with the Swiss cheese (the ham's heat will soften the cheese).

Spread the lettuce dressing on the top of the hoagie roll and add the tomato. Close the sandwich and serve.

✳ Carnitas

Roque's Carnitas is a chuckwagon that parks on Washington Street in Santa Fe, just around the corner from the *portale* of the Palace of the Governors, where Native Americans set up to sell jewelry. Dining here is as informal as can be. There are no white-clothed tables, no slick young waitstaff, no wine list, and no celebrity chef cleverly reinventing southwestern cuisine. Pay a few dollars and feast on a simple pleasure that no pretense could improve.

Only one meal is served: a sandwich made from a large, sturdy flour tortilla that has been heated on a grate over a charcoal fire. Inside is meat, and plenty of it: top round thinly sliced and seasoned in a garlic and soy sauce marinade. At the wagon, piles of this sopped beef are cooked on a grate over a hot open fire with sliced yellow onions and green chiles (New Mexican chiles when they are in season, in the fall; Anaheims the rest of the year). The mélange is tossed vigorously with tongs over the fire as the meat chars along its edges, engulfed in smoke, and the onions and peppers turn limp. Nearly a half-pound of this mixture is piled into the tortilla and topped with salsa. The hefty sandwich is tightly wrapped in foil so it can be carried without serious spillage.

It is a jolly mess. As soon as you peel back the foil and try to gather up the tortilla for eating, chunks of salsa tumble out, meat juice leaks, onions slither, and plump circles of earth-green chile pepper pop free. There is a tall garbage can near the carnitas wagon, and it is not unusual to see two or three well-dressed customers gathered around it, bending over at the waist and chomping on their sandwiches so that all the spillage falls right into the trash. The choice location for eating, though, is the plaza itself, on a bench. Here you can sit and lean far forward as you dine, thus sparing your shirt and your lap and providing the resident pigeons the carnitas banquet to which they are now accustomed.

The carnitas taste best when the meat and peppers are cooked over an open fire, but it is possible to prepare them in a hot skillet.

MAKES 4 LARGE CARNITAS

2	tablespoons minced fresh oregano
4	garlic cloves, minced
¼	cup soy sauce
¼	cup vegetable oil
¼	cup flat beer (lager)
1½	pounds top round or sirloin, sliced in thin strips against the grain
1	large onion, thinly sliced
5	fresh green chile peppers, sliced in rounds, with seeds
	(New Mexican chiles preferred; Anaheims are acceptable)
4	large flour tortillas, warmed
	Salsa (recipe follows)

Combine the oregano, garlic, soy sauce, oil, and beer in a small bowl. Put the beef in a large sealable plastic bag, add the marinade, and seal the bag, forcing out the air. Marinate the beef in the refrigerator for a minimum of 12 hours, preferably 24. Drain off the marinade and discard.

On a fine grate over an open fire or in a hot, lightly greased skillet, cook the meat, onion, and peppers, tossing them almost constantly, until the meat is well browned, about 5 minutes.

Use tongs to lift one quarter of the meat mixture from the grate or skillet, allowing any excess juice to drip away, and place it on a warm tortilla. Top with the salsa, fold the tortilla over, and wrap some aluminum foil around the sandwich to serve it. Serve immediately.

✳✳ Salsa

MAKES ABOUT 2 CUPS, ENOUGH FOR 4 CARNITAS

- 2 cups diced fresh tomatoes
- 2 garlic cloves, minced
- 6 jalapeño peppers, finely chopped
- 1 small onion, chopped
- 2 tablespoons chopped fresh cilantro (optional)

Combine all the ingredients in a medium bowl.

*✳ Catfish Po' Boy

MIDDENDORF'S ✳ AKERS, LOUISIANA

Barely saved from Hurricane Katrina by sandbag levees, Middendorf's is located among a ramshackle string of bait shops and crab vendors off the access road of Highway 51. Proprietors Joey and Susie Lamonte joke that their lack of tablecloths and candlelight has caused them to lose a few beans with New Orleans restaurant critics (who award beans rather than stars), but they have no interest in cloning, upscaling, or expanding the winning formula beyond an annex built next door for weekend and Mardi Gras overflow crowds. "I like the bright lights and Formica," Joey says. "I wouldn't know what to do with a dirty tablecloth."

The menu is a Cajun primer: early in the year, there are heaps of boiled spiced crawfish; warm weather means Manchac crabs; and while oysters are at their flavorful best in the "r" months, you can always have plush oyster stew and barbecued oysters on the half shell. The primary attraction is catfish. When Susie's grandmother, Josie Middendorf, opened for business in 1934, catfish was considered such a lowly dish that she didn't even name it on her menu. It was "the Middendorf Special."

Catfish dinners here can be had thick or thin, the thin catfish looking little like a whole catfish or even a standard-size catfish fillet. Breaded in cornmeal and fried, the ultra-thin strips knot into crunchy curlicues and bows like pale gold bunting piled high and tangled on a plate. The ribbons of white meat are startlingly moist, their catfish flavor cushioned by the envelope of crust to become mudpuppy in a minor key. You eat the thin catfish by hand, and once you pluck that first piece, there is no stopping until the plate is emptied.

But our subject here is sandwiches, and the fact is that there isn't a better catfish sandwich in this universe — or any other — than the one you'll have at Middendorf's. Here's the recipe, which Joey Lamonte calls Middendorf's Best Damn Catfish Po' Boy. Serve it with tangy coleslaw and a cold Barq's root beer.

Vegetable oil for deep-frying
8 5- to 6-inch catfish fillets
4 cups fine cornmeal (if too coarse, process in a food processor until fine)
4 8-inch lengths New Orleans–style soft-crusted French bread, or 4 hoagie rolls
Butter for spreading
Tartar Sauce (recipe follows)
Cocktail Sauce (recipe follows)
Optional additions: dill pickle chips, finely shredded lettuce, sliced tomatoes, hot sauce

Heat 3 to 4 inches of oil to 350 degrees in a deep-fat fryer or a large, deep skillet.

One at a time, dip the fillets in a bowl of lightly salted water, then quickly dredge them in the cornmeal. Carefully lay a small batch of fillets in the oil; do not crowd them. Fry, turning them once, until crispy, 6 to 7 minutes. Drain the catfish on paper towels. Repeat with the remaining fillets.

Meanwhile, preheat the broiler.

Slice the lengths of bread or the rolls in half horizontally and spread the insides with butter. Toast them under the broiler until light brown. Spread tartar sauce on each bottom piece of bread and cocktail sauce on the top pieces. Top each of the bottom halves with 2 hot catfish fillets. If desired, add dill pickle chips, lettuce, and tomatoes. A couple of drops of Louisiana hot sauce are also optional. Replace the tops of the bread, cut each sandwich in half, and serve.

✳ Tartar Sauce

- 1 cup mayonnaise
- 1 tablespoon finely chopped dill pickle
- 1 tablespoon minced onion
- 2 tablespoons fresh lemon juice
- 1 tablespoon finely chopped pitted green olives
- 1 garlic clove, finely minced

Mix all the ingredients in a small bowl.

✳ Cocktail Sauce

MAKES ABOUT 1 CUP, PLENTY FOR 4 LARGE SANDWICHES

- ½ cup chili sauce
- ½ cup ketchup
- 1 tablespoon prepared horseradish
- Dash of Worcestershire sauce

Mix all the ingredients in a small bowl.

Chicken Vesuvio

HARRY CARAY'S ✳ CHICAGO, ILLINOIS

Back in the 1920s in Chicago, a restaurant named Vesuvio's had such a renowned way with chicken that its recipe has since become one of the city's signature dishes: a heap of bone-in pieces of chicken that are sautéed, then baked until they are encased in a dark, red-gold crust of lush skin that slips from the meat as the meat slides off its bone. It is served on a plate piled with wedges of potato sautéed in a bath of white wine, garlic, olive oil, and spices until they are as soft as mashed inside, but with crunchy edges.

Our favorite place to eat chicken Vesuvio is Harry Caray's, a broad-shouldered steak house that is in every way the essence of Chicago. While you can get a classic plate of it for supper, the kitchen here also offers a chicken Vesuvio sandwich—a unique way of enjoying the hallmark flavor mix of the dish, but with the addition of Asiago cheese and tomatoes.

MAKES 4 SANDWICHES

- 4 boneless, skinless chicken breasts
- 1 teaspoon salt
- ½ teaspoon freshly ground pepper
- 2 teaspoons garlic powder
- 1 teaspoon dried oregano
- 1 teaspoon chopped fresh parsley
- ¼ cup olive oil
- ½ cup dry white wine
- ½ cup chicken stock (homemade or low-sodium canned broth)
- 4 ¼-inch-thick slices Asiago cheese
- 4 large focaccia buns or Italian rolls, sliced in half horizontally
- 4 leaves green-leaf lettuce
- 2 vine-ripened tomatoes, each cut into 4 slices

Season the chicken breasts with the salt, pepper, garlic powder, oregano, and parsley. Heat the oil in a large skillet over medium heat and cook the chicken breasts on both sides until golden brown, 2½ to 3 minutes per side.

Leaving the chicken in the pan, deglaze the pan with the wine, stirring to scrape up the browned bits. Add the stock and simmer, uncovered, for 20 to 25 minutes, or until the chicken is cooked to an internal temperature of 155 degrees.

Place a slice of Asiago cheese on each chicken breast and let it melt. Remove the chicken from the pan and place each breast on the bottom of a bun or roll. Top each breast with a lettuce leaf and 2 tomato slices. Take the tops of the buns and dip the cut sides in the remaining pan juices. Place on top of the sandwiches and serve.

✳ Chivito

The Olive Market is just five minutes from where we live. We shop there for cheeses, olives, and olive oil. We go there in the morning for strong coffee and frittatas, we go at lunch for sandwiches, and we go in the evening for spectacular dinners that reflect the Uruguayan roots of co-owner Fernando Pereyra. Fernando and his partner, Bill King, have made this cozy grocery store–café into a local hangout with something for everyone.

We love the grilled pizzas and the gaucho meat platters, and the Cuban sandwich you'll get here is excellent, but the one must-eat item on the menu is an unbelievably luxurious sandwich called the Chivito. This is a hot Uruguayan dagwood of so many different kinds of delicious protein that we have to think Dr. Atkins would have loved it (although a top-quality bakery roll is essential). Fernando's recipe suggests serving it with French fries, but when we dine at the Olive Market, we simply grab a bag of potato chips—and maybe a pitcher of sangria, too.

As for the hard roll, we recommend seeking out one with character. Especially well suited for a chivito are the Northeast's Portuguese rolls, Sheboygan (Wisconsin) bakery rolls, a small New Orleans muffuletta loaf, or any sturdy Italian torpedo.

MAKES 4 SANDWICHES

8 strips bacon
4 ¼-inch-thick slices filet mignon
  Salt and freshly ground pepper
4 large eggs
4 hard rolls (see headnote)
4 tablespoons mayonnaise
4 slices Black Forest ham
4 slices provolone cheese
  Lettuce
8 slices tomato
4 slices onion

Fry the bacon in a large skillet over medium-high heat, turning the strips once, until they are not quite crisp. Transfer the bacon to paper towels to drain, leaving the bacon grease in the skillet.

Pound each slice of filet mignon with a meat pounder until it is about the size of the hard roll. Salt and pepper the slices on both sides, then fry them in the bacon grease, turning them once, for 1 to 2 minutes. When they are cooked until pink in the center, remove the steaks. Fry the eggs in the remaining bacon grease, removing them when the yolks are cooked but still runny.

Meanwhile, slice the hard rolls and toast the cut sides. Spread mayonnaise on the cut side of each roll. On the bottom of each roll, place the filet mignon, followed by the ham, the provolone, a fried egg, 2 strips bacon, lettuce, 2 tomato slices, and an onion slice. Replace the tops and serve with many napkins.

✳ Chopped Liver

There is no better place in the world to enjoy a chopped liver sandwich than Katz's on Houston Street in New York. Houston Street used to be the border that divided the Jewish population of the Lower East Side from the rest of the world. It is now a polyglot melting pot, but many of the old Jewish culinary landmarks remain. Among them are Russ & Daughters for pickles, Yonah Schimmel's for knishes, and Katz's for a full range of kosher-style deli fare, including superb chopped liver sandwiches.

The recipe for a chopped liver sandwich is simplicity itself: schmear plenty of chopped liver on a slice of sour-crusted rye. Top with another slice of rye. Eat. This is one sandwich that needs no garnishes or condiments, and while some delis offer over-the-top variations that pair the chopped liver with pastrami or corned beef or turkey, most mavens like theirs plain.

Thus the secret of a great chopped liver sandwich is great chopped liver (and, of course, excellent rye bread). And the secret of great chopped liver is schmaltz. Schmaltz—rendered chicken fat—is to the Jewish cook what olive oil is to the Italian: the key ingredient in hundreds of recipes, the essential taste. Schmaltz also adds a silky texture.

It is possible to make your own schmaltz by boiling the subcutaneous fat from heavy chickens with a bit of water until the water is boiled away and the schmaltz is clear. But it takes a lot of fat chickens to make a little schmaltz, so all but the most perfectionistic cooks buy theirs at the deli or supermarket.

A food processor makes the process of putting together chopped liver extremely easy. One warning, though: touch the pulse button gingerly. You don't want your chopped liver too smooth. A grainy texture, with bits of unground liver, is best.

MAKES 4 LARGE SANDWICHES

1 pound beef livers
1 pound chicken livers
1/3 cup vegetable oil
1 large onion, sliced
2 eggs, hard-cooked (recipe follows)
1 teaspoon salt
1/2 teaspoon freshly ground pepper
6 tablespoons schmaltz (see headnote)
8 slices rye bread

Preheat the broiler.

Place the beef livers on the rack of a broiler pan and broil until they are cooked through but not dried out (there's no need to turn them), about 10 minutes. Broil the chicken livers in the same pan.

Heat the oil in a small skillet over medium heat and sauté the onion until it is soft, about 4 minutes.

Combine the livers, onion, oil in which the onion was cooked, and hard-cooked eggs in a food processor. Process very briefly to mix the ingredients. Add the salt, pepper, and schmaltz. Blend until you achieve a rugged, pasty texture.

Transfer the mixture to a bowl, cover, and cool in the refrigerator. The chopped liver will stiffen as it cools.

Divide the chopped liver among the bottom slices of bread, cap with the top slices, and serve.

Hard-Cooked Eggs

Place the eggs in a small saucepan of cold water. Bring to a boil and boil for 1 minute. Remove from the heat, cover, and let stand for 15 minutes. Drain, cover with cold water for a few minutes, then peel under cold running water.

KATZ'S

Katz's has been a part of New York's Lower East Side since 1888. A big painted sign outside offers the enigmatic slogan "Katz's — That's All!" the meaning of which eludes most people. Here's the story: Many years ago, when the proprietor decided he needed a new sign, the sign painter he hired asked him what he wanted the sign to say. The proprietor replied with the obvious: "Katz's."

"Nothing else?" the painter asked, yearning to have a little more to work with.

Slightly exasperated, the owner answered, "Katz's — that's all." And that is what he got.

Inside, this relic of bygone New York operates like an old-time urban deli: you get a ticket when you enter, and as you order food at the counter, the ticket is marked accordingly. Pay on your way out.

It is a cavernous eating hall with lined-up tables, the air filled with the noise of shouted orders and clattering carving knives and the aroma of the odoriferous garlicky salamis hanging along the wall. Pictures of happy celebrity customers, ranging from comics Jerry Lewis and Henny Youngman to Police Commissioner Raymond Kelly, are everywhere.

For a greenhorn, merely getting food at Katz's can be an intimidating process. Ordinary table service by waiters is available, and quite easy. But that is the coward's way. To earn your stripes at Katz's, you must personally engage wits with a counterman. To do that, you take your ticket to the nose-high counter and make eye contact with one of the white-aproned carvers who is busy slicing meats and making sandwiches behind the glass. Once you've gotten his attention, quickly tell him what you want: pastrami on rye or on a club roll, or corned beef, or brisket. Not one of these guys would win a Mr. Congeniality contest, but they do their job with the certainty and expertise of a Dutch diamond cutter.

When the meat is cut (all by hand, of course) and the sandwich assembled, it is plated with a pickle. The counterman uses a grease pencil to mark its cost on the ticket you received on the way in. You then carry the plate and ticket to the far end of the counter for French fries or a Dr. Brown's Cel-Ray soda, or to the near end for an egg cream, where the ticket is marked up accordingly by the staff. Then carry your food to a table and feast.

Even if you don't enjoy the attitude (we find it fun, as if Don Rickles were a restaurant), all is forgiven when you heft a Katz's pastrami sandwich: three-quarters of a pound of meat that has been expertly severed into pieces so chunky that the word "slice" seems too lightweight to describe them. Each brick-red, glistening, moist hunk is rimmed black, redolent of garlic, smoke, and pickling spices, as savory as food can be. You can pay a dollar more to have it cut extra-lean, but it is hard to imagine these taut, pink slices any leaner than they are.

"We go through five thousand pounds of pastrami every week," says owner Alan Dell, who happens to stroll by our table and stop when he hears us groaning with delight over his delicious sandwiches. Apparently our rapture is so audible that he compares us to the pros and says, "What, you're not sitting at the *When Harry Met Sally* table?" He points to the one at which actress Meg Ryan did her show-stopping fake-orgasm scene while eating Katz's food. "You know, I counted: Billy Crystal ate six pastrami sandwiches when they filmed that," Mr. Dell reports. "And between sandwiches, he was at the counter eating hot dogs." (Although we missed sitting at Meg and Billy's table, we did manage to secure seats at the one where a hand-lettered sign advises: "You are sitting at the table where Vice Pres. Gore and the Prime Minister of Russia had their deli summit lunch.")

Mr. Dell, wearing a Katz's souvenir shirt that implores "Send a Salami to Your Boy in the Army," engages us in a Socratic dialogue about pastrami's roots. "Who invented it?" he asks.

"Romanians," we say — the traditional history-book answer.

"And why?"

"Pickling and smoking are ways of preserving meat without refrigeration." Again we give the standard explanation.

"Aha!" he says, raising a forefinger in the air. "Who else preserved meat that way? Who else didn't have refrigerators?"

We are stumped.

"American Indians!" he says. "That's the new twist. They invented pastrami, long before Jews came to America." As we marvel at the theory, Mr. Dell adds in a low voice, "Of course, they had no rye bread or pickle." He then seamlessly segues into a monologue about all the TV shows and movies that have come to Katz's because it offers such a colorful slice of city life. Before strolling away to schmooze with other customers, he offers a grand finale to his recitation: "If it's New York you want, Katz's is the spot!"

✳ Chow Mein

EVELYN'S DRIVE-IN ✳ TIVERTON, RHODE ISLAND

The chow mein sandwich, a strange specialty of drive-ins and cafés mostly on the south coast of Massachusetts and Rhode Island east of Narragansett Bay, exists because Frederick Wong started the Oriental Chow Mein Company in 1936. Genuine chow mein sandwiches are built with the noodles the family makes at the old building in Fall River, Massachusetts. These noodles are crunchy, not soft as in chow mein elsewhere, and traditional chow mein sandwiches hereabouts are meatless: simply noodles topped with sauced vegetables and sprouts, all on a plate along with a hamburger bun.

For those of us more familiar with typical Chinese-American chow mein, the concept is a little weird. It is certainly not a sandwich you can pick up and eat, and while a bun floating in chow mein at first seems anomalous, the eater soon discovers that it is a mighty handy tool for mopping up the last of the gravy from the plate.

At Evelyn's Drive-In you will not want a plate. The way to eat a chow mein sandwich here—where it is served only Monday through Thursday—is out of a disposable Styrofoam clamshell container. This makes sense, especially in nice weather, because Evelyn's best eating facilities are outdoor picnic tables (there is an inside dining room, too). From one of these breezy seats (under a covered pavilion), you have a view of the water and are serenaded by screeching seagulls.

We're going to assume that most readers do not have access to Oriental Chow Mein Company noodles, which are marketed locally with the brand name Hoo-Mee, so the following recipe includes directions for frying your own.

MAKES 4 SANDWICHES

1   pound dried Chinese egg noodles
    Vegetable oil for deep-frying
1   quart chicken stock, homemade preferred
¼ cup cornstarch
2   tablespoons vegetable oil
2   celery stalks, cut into ¼-inch slices
1   large sweet onion, cut in half and sliced into strips (not rings)
2   garlic cloves, minced
1   cup bean sprouts
¼ cup molasses
4   hamburger buns

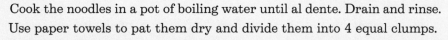

Cook the noodles in a pot of boiling water until al dente. Drain and rinse. Use paper towels to pat them dry and divide them into 4 equal clumps.

Heat 3 to 4 inches of oil to 350 degrees in a deep-fryer or a large saucepan. Using a slotted spoon, lower a clump of noodles into the oil and fry, turning it once, until crisp and brown, about 5 minutes. Drain well on paper towels. Repeat with the remaining batches.

Make a paste by mixing 1 cup of the chicken stock with the cornstarch in a small bowl.

Heat the 2 tablespoons vegetable oil in a deep cast-iron skillet or wok. Add the celery, onion, and garlic and cook until they start to soften, about 2 minutes. Add the bean sprouts and cook for 1 more minute, until they begin to get limp. Stir in the remaining 3 cups chicken stock. Then stir in the cornstarch mixture, stirring constantly as the mixture thickens. Add the molasses, stir a few more times, and remove the skillet from the heat.

Separate the hamburger buns into tops and bottoms and place both sides in four deep plates. Top one side of the bun with one of the fried noodle batches. Top the other side with one fourth of the bean sprout mixture. Repeat with the other buns. Serve immediately—with utensils!

✳ Clam Roll

CLAM BOX ✳ IPSWICH, MASSACHUSETTS

If you haven't eaten fried clams on the North Shore of Massachusetts, you haven't eaten fried clams. And if you want the best of the best, the place to go is the Clam Box of Ipswich. Open for business since 1935, the Clam Box is shaped like the kind of cardboard box that is used to serve orders of fried clams at eat-in-the-rough restaurants along Yankee shores. It is 15 by 15 feet at the bottom, a little wider at the top, and 30 feet high. Since the Box was built, inside dining space has been added around the bottom of the jumbo container, diluting the trompe l'oeil effect of seventy years ago, but it is still a striking roadside attraction. The interior and exterior of this amazing place are impeccable: there are pretty flower boxes all around the outside, and the booths, tables, and captain's chairs are varnished and shiny.

While many kinds of fried seafood (and even nonfried items) are available, it is clams that put this place on the map. They are lightly cooked, so each one comes sheathed in a frail crust that yearns to blend with the clam inside. They have a lively salt-sea character, and according to Marina ("Chickie") Aggelakis, the proprietor, the primary secret is using clean oil for frying. When we asked Chickie for a recipe, she recommended Crisco or canola oil; some clam chefs in the area insist that the oil must contain some lard. It is also vital that the clams be freshly shucked soft-shells — the kind that are harvested from clam beds thereabouts. Frozen clams are not acceptable. Shucked ones are available in seafood markets; shucking them is a job for professionals.

The typical way to have fried clams is on a plate with fried onion rings and French fried potatoes, as well as sweet coleslaw and a small buttered bun that is useful for scooping the last of the tartar sauce out of the small cup in which it is served. A clam roll condenses the formula, and may even improve it: a good toasted and buttered bun is such an excellent foil for the crunchy nuggets of marine succulence.

MAKES 6 CLAM ROLLS

Crisco oil or canola oil for deep-frying
Butter, softened, for brushing rolls

6   split-top hot dog buns
3   cups corn flour (also known as masa harina, available in Latino markets)
1   cup pastry flour or white cake flour
1   large can evaporated milk (1²/₃ cups)
1   quart freshly shucked soft-shell clams
     Tartar Sauce (recipe follows)

In a deep-fat fryer or a large, deep skillet, heat 3 to 4 inches of oil to 350 degrees. Butter the outside of the hot dog buns and toast both sides on a griddle. Keep warm in the oven. Mix the corn flour and pastry flour in a large bowl. Pour the evaporated milk into a large shallow bowl.

Dip the clams into the evaporated milk. Strain off the excess liquid and then dredge the clams in the flour mixture, working with no more than ½ cup clams at a time. Shake off the excess flour and drop the clams into the hot oil; do not crowd them. Cook, turning them, until the clams are golden brown, about 2 minutes. Remove with a slotted spoon and drain on paper towels. Pile the hot clams onto the toasted rolls and serve immediately, with tartar sauce on the side.

Tartar Sauce

MAKES 1 CUP

¼   cup diced onion
¼   cup drained sweet relish
½   cup mayonnaise

Mix all the ingredients in a small bowl.

✳ Cortland

MAGNOLIA'S ✳ CARMEL, NEW YORK

New York is apple country. Look behind Magnolia's restaurant from the late summer into fall. There you will see the tree from which K.C. Scott and her two right hands in the kitchen, JoAnn and Mimi, take unsprayed apples to can jars of applesauce and apple butter. "We like the old favorites like the Cortland and the Macoun," K.C. told us. She took the apples from her tree to an orchard owner, but he was unable to identify exactly what kind they are. "Perhaps an heirloom variety," she surmises.

The little restaurant K.C. and her friends operate is an adorable Putnam County spot that is part of a house facing scenic Lake Gleneida. Indoor seats and a scattering of tables on a small patio offer a view of Route 6 and the water. Barbecued pork and brisket are smoked out on the patio, and in cooler months the kitchen turns its attention to spectacularly good handmade truffles, caramels, nut crunches, and, in K.C.'s words, "anything else I feel like coating with chocolate."

The service is supremely informal: order at the counter, grab your beverage from the cooler to the left, and the staff brings your meal to the table when it's ready. This is our kind of eating experience: quick, breezy, inexpensive, and good-tasting.

Starting at seven in the morning, you can go to Magnolia's for an omelet, French toast, pancakes, an egg-potato-cheese-salsa burrito, or waffles (weekends only).

While the hot-meal repertoire has expanded over the years and salads are huge, Magnolia's sandwiches are what first won our hearts. A blackboard lists specials; the regular repertoire includes a Local Hero, portobello mushroom and pepper sandwich on focaccia bread, and a Ludington, a grilled cheddar cheese and tomato sandwich on hearth bread. We are particularly fond of two always-available wraps: the Catalina, which is an assortment of vegetables, including delicious roasted peppers, in an herb wrap, and the Cortland, grilled chicken and Havarti cheese sweetened with nuggets of locally grown Cortland apple, all drizzled with a tangy, pepper-speckled dressing.

(NOTE: In January 2007, Magnolia's moved to Patterson, New York.)

MAKES 4 WRAPS

4 slices Havarti cheese with dill
3 4- to 5-ounce grilled or roasted chicken breasts, cut into bite-size pieces
1 apple (Cortland or other firm variety), cut into small pieces
8 large leaves red-leaf lettuce or a handful of mesclun greens
8 large slices tomato
4 large (13-inch) sun-dried tomato wraps
²/₃ cup Parmesan Peppercorn Dressing, homemade (recipe follows)
or store-bought

For each sandwich, layer the ingredients across the center of the wrap and drizzle with 2 to 3 tablespoons of the Parmesan dressing. Fold the bottom third of the wrap up over the filling and fold the sides in toward the center. Roll the rest of the way, tucking in the sides as you roll. Serve.

Parmesan Peppercorn Dressing

Good bottled Parmesan peppercorn dressings are available, but here is a quick food-processor recipe to make your own.

MAKES ABOUT 2¹/₂ CUPS

1 cup sour cream
1 cup buttermilk
²/₃ cup finely grated Parmesan cheese
1 garlic clove, minced
¹/₃ cup white wine vinegar
2 tablespoons coarsely ground pepper
Salt (optional)

Place all the ingredients except the salt in a food processor and blend until fairly smooth. Taste, and add salt if desired. Place in a well-sealed container and refrigerate for 1 to 2 hours before using. (The dressing will keep, covered and refrigerated, for up to a week.)

✳ Crab Bruschetta

BREAD AND INK CAFE ✳ PORTLAND, OREGON

The Hawthorne neighborhood of Portland has a surfeit of restaurants, many of them new. Bread and Ink is by now an old-timer, and a favorite destination eatery for us whenever we come to town. It is an unusual place, featuring great blintzes at its Yiddish brunch on Sunday and a diverse menu that includes Vietnamese spring rolls, Italian wedding cake, and some of the best hamburgers on the West Coast (served on a warm onion bun with homemade condiments).

There are two ways we like to start a meal here: with an arugula and hazelnut-crusted chèvre salad or with chef Mary Fishback's wonderful open-faced sandwich of baked Dungeness crab. Be sure to make these luscious treats on really good baguette bread, and of course, the fresher and sweeter the crabmeat is, the better they will taste.

MAKES 12 OPEN-FACED SANDWICHES; SERVES 6 AS AN APPETIZER OR 3 AS A MEAL

- ½ pound jumbo lump crabmeat, picked over for shells and cartilage
- 3 tablespoons chopped fresh basil
- ⅓ cup chopped roasted red bell peppers (see page 89)
- 2 scallions, thinly sliced
- ¾ cup grated Parmesan cheese
- ½ cup mayonnaise
- 3 tablespoons Wasabi Aïoli (recipe follows)
- 2 teaspoons fresh lemon juice
- ¼ teaspoon red pepper flakes
- 12 slices baguette bread, toasted
- ⅓ cup pine nuts
- Lemon wedges

Preheat the oven to 450 degrees.

In a large bowl, combine all the ingredients except the bread, pine nuts, and lemon wedges. Mix well. Spread the mixture evenly on the 12 slices of toast. Sprinkle the top of each with a few pine nuts. Place on a baking sheet and bake until brown and bubbly, about 5 minutes.

Serve with lemon wedges alongside.

Wasabi Aïoli

MAKES 1 CUP

- 2 garlic cloves
- 3 tablespoons wasabi paste (mix wasabi powder with water or buy prepared paste)
- 1 tablespoon unseasoned rice vinegar
  Pinch of salt
- 2 large egg yolks
- ¼ cup olive oil
- ¾ cup canola oil

Place the garlic, wasabi paste, vinegar, salt, and egg yolks in a food processor. With the processor running, start to add the oils in a very thin stream (do not add too much at a time or the mayo will curdle). When you have added about a third of the oil, continue adding it in a slightly thicker stream, being careful not to add too much too quickly.

Any leftover aïoli will keep for up to a week, refrigerated and covered.

Crab Cake (The Richard Colburn)

CHICK & RUTH'S DELLY ✳ ANNAPOLIS, MARYLAND

Being near the District of Columbia, Chick & Ruth's Delly has its own twist on the kosher-style-restaurant theme of giving celebrity monikers to sandwiches. Here the house specialties carry the names of politicians ranging from President George W. Bush (grilled Swiss, tomato, and bacon on rye) to George Nutwell, who is billed as the registrar of wills (corned beef and Swiss on rye).

The traditional deli-meat sandwiches at Chick & Ruth's are fantastic, but as satisfying as the regular-size ones are, the menu offers a special section called "The Biggest Sandwiches in Annapolis," for which corned beef, pastrami, salami, turkey, roast beef, and/or ham are piled ridiculously high on rye. We have never ordered but are immensely intrigued by one blockbuster titled "U.S.S. Annapolis (Nuclear Fast Attack Submarine): eighteen inches of baked-here bread heaped with hams, salamis, cheese, lettuce, tomato, onions, and a special Italian sauce."

Less likely specialties of the house include barbecued ribs, fried shrimp, extra-thick milk shakes, and great crab cakes. "I know most people don't think of crab cakes when they think about good deli food," said Teddy Levitt, whose father started the business in 1965. "But this is crab country. We get the best crab, and I believe we make the best cakes." They are available on a surf-and-turf platter with a T-bone steak, or in a seafood combo with fried clams and fried shrimp, or in a sandwich named for Richard Colburn, who has been a Maryland state senator since 1995.

Mr. Levitt told us that the secret of a great crab cake, other than excellent crabmeat from the nearby Chesapeake Bay, is cooking it quickly. "The longer you take, the greater the chance it will dry out," he explained. Baked, broiled, or fried, crab cakes demand the highest possible temperature so the outside browns well and the inside merely warms enough to cook the egg.

1   large egg

1   teaspoon Old Bay seasoning

1   teaspoon Worcestershire sauce

1   tablespoon prepared mustard (Dijon if desired)

1½ tablespoons mayonnaise

1   pound jumbo lump crabmeat, picked over for shells and cartilage

¼ cup finely chopped fresh bread crumbs

    Butter, or clarified butter (see page 152) if frying crab cakes

    Tartar Sauce (optional; page 39 or 51)

4   kaiser rolls

4   leaves lettuce

4   slices tomato

Beat the egg in a small bowl and mix in the Old Bay seasoning, Worcestershire sauce, mustard, and mayonnaise.

Place the crabmeat in a separate bowl and sprinkle with the bread crumbs. Gently mix. Then add the egg mixture, folding it in by hand. Be careful not to overmix.

Gently form the mixture into 4 crab cakes.

Preheat the broiler if you are planning to broil the crab cakes, or preheat the oven to the maximum temperature if you want to bake them.

To fry, melt the butter in a large skillet, add the crab cakes, and cook, turning them once, until the outside is light gold and the interior is hot, 2 to 4 minutes. If baking, melt the butter in a baking pan and bake the crab cakes for 5 to 6 minutes (no need to turn them). To broil, butter the broiler pan rack and broil, turning once, for 4 to 5 minutes. Do not overcook.

Spread tartar sauce over the top half of each kaiser roll if desired. Place a hot crab cake on the bottom half of each roll. Add lettuce and tomato, cover with the top half of the roll, and serve.

Crab Salad Roll

RED'S EATS ✳ WISCASSET, MAINE

A couple of years ago a contributor to the Roadfood.com Regional Eats Forum expressed this opinion:

> Lobster rolls seem to always take center stage as the classic Down East roadside delicacy. This unfairly draws attention away from another uniquely (and arguably more perfect) Maine gustatory delight—the humble and elegant Maine crab salad roll, which is a split-type hot dog roll butter-grilled and stuffed with fresh hand-picked local crab, mixed lightly with mayonnaise. A slice of iceberg lettuce is forgivable but not preferred. Nothing should interfere with the cool, fresh taste of crab. The buttery crunch, the soft "give" of the grilled white bread roll, and the mayo-enhanced crab make for a classic nosh amidst the pointed firs and rocky coasts of Maine.

Amen, friend! We confess our own guilt, always going for the lobster roll. But spurred by the admonition, we went to Red's Eats in Wiscasset, home of perhaps the greatest lobster roll on the coast, and for once did not eat only lobster. Sure enough, the crab roll was a magnificent meal, every bit as large and lavish as the lobster roll.

Since then we have become acutely aware that Maine is the fried-stuff-in-a-roll state, where many menus offer not only lobster rolls, crab rolls, and clam rolls, but also scallop rolls and shrimp rolls. Red's Eats even lists a chicken roll on its menu. A few such rolls come on hamburger buns, but the classic Maine version is piled into a split-top hot dog bun, the kind you can grill in butter on both sides so it develops a crisp, golden skin while the white inside, where the seafood goes, retains its softness. One other primary difference among Maine's crab rolls is what the crab is mixed with. A few places use Miracle Whip; among those where mayonnaise rules, there is strong brand loyalty to either Hellmann's or Cains. Some crab salads contain little bits of celery, pickle, or onion—more for crunch than for taste. Fresh-picked crabmeat is essential. Rock crabs (known as peekytoes) are what most Mainers use.

⅓ cup mayonnaise

¼ cup finely chopped celery or, if preferred, pickle (sweet or sour, to taste)

1 tablespoon finely chopped onion

½ cup fresh crabmeat, picked over for shells and cartilage

Butter

2 split-top hot dog buns, or 4 thick slices good white bread

2-4 leaves iceberg lettuce

Freshly ground pepper (optional)

Mix the mayonnaise with the celery or pickle and the onion. Gently stir in the crabmeat, but try not to break it up.

Heat a large skillet and add butter to taste. Brown both sides of the buns. (If using bread, brown only one side of each slice. It is imperative that the crab salad be cosseted in the soft part of the bread.) Remove the buns from the skillet and layer on a leaf or two of lettuce. Top the lettuce with the crab salad. Season with freshly ground pepper if desired.

✳ Cuban Mix

EL SIBONEY ✳ KEY WEST, FLORIDA

The ingredients of a Cuban mix necessarily include cheese and at least two kinds of pork. It is made in a length of Cuban bread, and most distinctive of all, it is grilled in a sandwich press so that the ingredients nearly fuse and the bread turns crisp. Thus, although it has the same basic architecture as a po' boy or a Delaware Valley hoagie, it is usually tidy enough to hoist in one hand with little fear of collapse.

Nobody knows for sure who made the first one, but the best explanation we have heard is that immigrants from Cuba who settled in the Ybor City part of Tampa over a hundred years ago were the first to popularize it. "El Cubano" is now an immensely popular sandwich in Tampa and throughout southern Florida, as well as in several hole-in-the-wall diners in New York City.

You won't find a better Cuban mix than the one served at El Siboney, a happy-go-lucky café with red-striped tablecloths outfitted with silverware presented in tidy little paper bags. It's a favorite gathering place of Spanish-speaking locals, but if you don't savvy Español, the waitresses do their best to help you understand the menu. Ours explained that El Siboney was a Cuban Indian and that the name of the place and the Indian-themed art on the walls are a tribute to him.

El Siboney's Cuban mix is ham, roast pork, Swiss cheese, and garlicky salami dressed with pickles, lettuce, and tomato. The meats are sliced thin and layered neatly so that the sandwich makers can cut each warm, crisp-crusted sandwich at a rakish angle, revealing beautiful, complex cross sections of all the ingredients.

If you can get fresh Cuban bread for this sandwich (made with lard and therefore almost instantly perishable), that's great. If not, Italian or French bread makes a good substitute. And if you don't have a plancha (that's the sandwich press so essential in the Cuban restaurant kitchen), the sandwich can be toasted in a frying pan with a heavy iron weight, such as another frying pan, on top of it. If you're doing it this way, it is important to flip the sandwich after a few minutes so both top and bottom get totally toasty.

5 sandwich-size slices ham
2 slices roast pork
2 slices garlicky salami
1 long slice Swiss cheese
1 8-inch length Cuban bread (see headnote), cut in half lengthwise
1-2 leaves lettuce
2-3 slices tomato
  Dill pickle chips to taste
  Mustard to taste
  Mayonnaise to taste

Layer the meats and cheese on the bottom half of the bread, topping with the lettuce, tomato, pickles, and condiments of choice. Place the sandwich in a hot press (see headnote) and cook until the cheese is melted and the ingredients are nearly fused, 7 to 8 minutes. Serve hot.

✳✳ Debbie's Hot Pork Roast

ANN SATHER ✳✳ CHICAGO, ILLINOIS

If truth be told, we used to think of Ann Sather's only for breakfast. Delicious cinnamon rolls, common one state over in Iowa, are rare in Illinois. But the rolls served in this neighborhood coffee shop are ravishing. You get two goopy-good rolls per order, each blanketed in a sweet sugar glaze. The menu lists seven versions of eggs Benedict: steak, turkey, smoked salmon, creamed spinach, crab cakes, fresh tomato, or ham. And there are omelets, biscuits, muffins, and homemade Swedish rye bread for toast. The Swedish pancakes are legendary, and we love the waffles, which are thin and crisp and elegant.

After years of feasting on such morning meals, we came to Ann Sather's one day for lunch. What a revelation! We had two great hot sandwiches: one held fetchingly sweet Swedish meatballs, the other roast pork. The latter in particular caused us to grin from ear to ear (and made a necessity of returning for a dinner of roast loin of pork with caraway-seed sauerkraut). The pork itself was delicious, but we were smitten with its rich sausage gravy.

This is a sandwich that requires you to sit down to eat with a knife and fork. We like to serve it with mashed potatoes and chunky applesauce.

MAKES 6 MEAL-SIZE OPEN-FACE SANDWICHES

    Roast Pork (recipe follows)
6   thick slices hearty white bread
    Sausage Sour Cream Gravy (recipe follows)

Slice the roast pork. Place 1 slice of white bread on each plate and top with slices of the roast pork (about 1 inch high). Pour on the gravy to taste and serve.

✳✳ Roast Pork

1	4-pound boneless pork roast, loin or center-cut
2	garlic cloves, minced
	Salt and freshly ground pepper to taste
4	bay leaves
½	cup white vinegar
½	teaspoon dried thyme

Preheat the oven to 325 degrees.

Pierce the roast in several places with a two-pronged fork and force some of the minced garlic into each hole, using the fork to push it in. Sprinkle the roast liberally with salt and pepper. Place the bay leaves in the bottom of a roasting pan. Place the roast on top, fat side up. Combine the vinegar and thyme and pour it evenly over the roast. Place the pan in the oven and cook, basting occasionally, until an instant-read thermometer registers 150 degrees, about 2 hours.

✳✳ Sausage Sour Cream Gravy

MAKES ABOUT 12 CUPS

5	cups water
3	cups milk
1	pound loose pork sausage (not links)
1½	cups all-purpose flour
2	tablespoons salt
2	tablespoons freshly ground pepper
3	cups sour cream

Mix the water and milk in a large pot and place over low heat; do not boil.

In a large skillet, cook the sausage, stirring to break it up and keep it loose-textured. When it is browned, lift it out with a slotted spoon and add it to the water and milk. Strain the grease and return it to the skillet.

Stir the flour, salt, and pepper into the grease to make a roux. Cook over medium heat until it thickens and clings to a spoon and pours from the skillet cleanly. When the milk and water mixture is just about to boil, stir the sausage roux into it to thicken the gravy and turn off the heat. Stir in the sour cream.

Use leftover gravy to top morning biscuits.

Diana's Different Drummer (Brisket on Rye)

ZINGERMAN'S DELI ⁂ ANN ARBOR, MICHIGAN

In the twenty-five years since it opened in an old building near the farmers' market, Zingerman's has grown to become one of America's great delis and a source of countless magnificent sandwiches (not to mention a mail-order bounty available by catalog and at www.zingermans.com). One of the best sandwiches on the menu is a bonanza of brisket, Russian dressing, and coleslaw called Diana's Different Drummer. Proprietor Ari Weinzweig told us that the sandwich was named for Diana Dobry, whose husband was the drummer in a local cult rock favorite, Destroy All Monsters.

According to Ari, "The better the raw brisket you start with, the better-tasting the finished product." He described the magic of this particular sandwich as a balance, with "the warm, juicy texture of the meat offset nicely by the cool crunch of the coleslaw and the Russian dressing. And the richness of the rest of the ingredients is accented by the heat of the horseradish."

MAKES 2 HUGE SANDWICHES

- 4 slices rye bread
- 2 tablespoons grated or prepared horseradish
- ¼ cup Russian Dressing (recipe follows)
- ⅓ cup coleslaw
- 8 ounces sliced cooked beef brisket (available at any good Jewish deli)

Cover 2 slices of the bread with the horseradish, spreading it to the edges. Spread 2 tablespoons of the Russian dressing over each of those slices, mixing it in with the horseradish. Top the undressed slices with the coleslaw and brisket. Add the other pieces of bread, cut the sandwiches in half diagonally, and eat up!

Russian Dressing

MAKES 2 CUPS

- ³/₄ cup mayonnaise
- ¹/₄ cup plus 2–3 tablespoons chili sauce
- 2 tablespoons sour cream
- 2 teaspoons chopped fresh curly-leaf parsley
- 1 tablespoon plus 1 teaspoon minced Spanish onion
- 1 tablespoon plus 1 teaspoon minced dill pickle
- ¹/₂ teaspoon fresh lemon juice
- ¹/₂ teaspoon grated or prepared horseradish
- ¹/₄ teaspoon Worcestershire sauce

Combine all the ingredients in a small bowl and mix well.

Egg McDot Deluxe

DOT'S RESTAURANT ✳ WILMINGTON, VERMONT

If there are small towns in heaven, every one will have a place like Dot's: open for three square meals a day starting before dawn, with a staff of seasoned pros who are as welcoming to strangers passing through as to everyday regulars. The building itself—on Main Street, of course—has character galore. It was built in 1832 and has been a post office and a retail store. Current proprietors John and Patty Reagan told us, "We believe it started operating as a restaurant sometime after the turn of the twentieth century."

Dot's is a favorite of skiers on their way to or from Mount Snow, and there's no place better to stop for a really hearty breakfast. We love the kitchen's French toast, made with cracked-wheat bread; the berry-berry pancakes, poured of a batter positively loaded with blackberries, strawberries, raspberries, and blueberries; and the McDot's breakfast sandwiches, which are based on the yellow arches' but are really, really good.

Every McDot is made to order, and so the possible combinations are vast. You can have your egg cooked any way from hard-as-rubber to runny enough to spill down your chin when bitten; you can add bacon, ham, hot sausage, sweet sausage, Canadian bacon, sliced turkey, a whole hamburger, corned beef hash, even Dot's renowned jailhouse chili. Cheese choices include American, Swiss, and Vermont cheddar, and bread possibilities range from toasted and buttered English muffins to that wonderful cracked-wheat bread used for their French toast. "If it's in the house, we will put it in your sandwich," the Reagans promise.

The most spectacular variation is the McDot Deluxe, which the menu bills as "Double the Dot, Double the Cholesterol." We suggest having this after a morning of skiing or other vigorous activity. The recipe for our favorite combo follows.

MAKES ONE 8-INCH SANDWICH

4   strips maple-smoked bacon
2   tablespoons butter, plus more for roll
2   large eggs
1   grinder roll, about 8 inches long
¼   cup grated mild Vermont cheddar cheese

Cook the bacon in a large skillet, turning it once, until not quite crisp. Drain on paper towels. Remove the grease from the pan (although leaving a film of it will add flavor). Melt the butter and crack the eggs into the skillet. Fry them as you like. (Breaking the yolks in the pan will avoid a seriously drippy sandwich.)

Meanwhile, split the roll lengthwise, butter the inside, and toast it in a large cast-iron skillet or on a griddle just long enough to get the inside slightly crisp. Remove the roll from the heat and immediately sprinkle the cheese across the bottom half so the heat of the roll softens and begins to melt the cheese. Remove the eggs from the pan with a spatula and place them on top of the cheese; their heat will continue the melting process. Layer the bacon on top of the eggs and place the top half of the roll on the sandwich. Serve hot.

Elvis Special

He sold over a billion records and his face is as familiar as the sun, but of all the Elvis superlatives, nothing was grander than his appetite. It was immense—perhaps the most famous appetite in history, certainly the best-known since that other insatiable king, Henry VIII.

Elvis's talent for packing away food has become part of his legend, and like so much else about the fairy-tale life of the skinny boy who went from a shotgun shack in Tupelo, Mississippi, to the leopardskin-and-gold-trimmed cocoon of Graceland, it's hard to know where fact ends and tall tales begin. Did he really eat two pounds of bacon at a sitting? Were eight well-done hamburgers and three malts a typical lunch?

Living large was the rockabilly king's credo. He consumed too much of everything he liked: bacon, banana yogurt, honeydew melons, Spanish omelets, and peanut-and-chocolate-topped ice cream cones. When he was young it didn't matter, because he burned calories by the thousand every night. But then, as happens to us all, his metabolism slowed. In fact, Elvis had a weight problem most of his adult life, which he spent alternately feasting and dieting.

That's one reason many El-Fans love him and feel so close to him. He ate like a regular guy, with a restless appetite that had once known what it was like to go hungry. His waistline was proof that no matter how regal his life became, he remained a good old boy with a weakness for burgers. From his suite atop the Las Vegas Hilton, where any whim, however outlandish, could be satisfied, he sent out for bags of them, because the hotel kitchen's filet mignon didn't suit his fancy. At home when he grew hungry in the middle of the night, he sat at the kitchen table dipping hunks of corn bread into buttermilk long enough for each piece to become what he called a "soak"—a big, soft mouthful of earthy tenderness. And he taught every maid at Graceland exactly how to make the snack he liked best: a grilled peanut butter and banana sandwich. This was the kind of comfort food his beloved mother, Gladys, used to cook for him—food with the down-home country soul that made him a people's king.

The proper beverage to serve with this is buttermilk.

70

SANDWICHES

2 tablespoons peanut butter (smooth is preferred)
2 slices fresh white bread
1 small ripe banana, freshly mashed to a pulp
2 tablespoons butter or margarine

Spread the peanut butter on 1 slice of bread. Spread the mashed banana on the other. Gently press the 2 slices together.

Melt the butter or margarine in a small frying pan over medium-low heat. Fry the sandwich on one side until golden brown. Flip and fry the other side.

Eat by hand (this can be messy) or with a knife and fork.

Ferdi's Special

MOTHER'S ✳ NEW ORLEANS, LOUISIANA

When Mother's reopened a month after Hurricane Katrina struck, there were not enough remaining staff members to wash dishes. So they used Styrofoam—and served the usual paradigmatic New Orleans fare.

Today Mother's is what it has been since it opened in 1938: a blue-plate lunchroom where for a few dollars New Orleanians from every rung of the social ladder come to feast. Morning grits are usually available with debris, pronounced "*day*-bree," which is all the pieces of beef that fall into the gravy when a roast is carved. At lunch, in addition to definitive po' boy sandwiches, Mother's is known for gumbo (Wednesday), red beans and rice (Tuesday), jambalaya, spaghetti pie, and bread pudding with brandy sauce for dessert.

It's an everyday place where everybody waits in the cafeteria line and the staff treats them all with nonchalant disrespect. If you are going for lunch, we recommend visiting early. The first lunchtime customers have the opportunity to avail themselves of a lagniappe, such as cracklin's from the "black ham"—little amber squiggles and crusty sweet chunks from the outside of the baked meat—which are a brilliant addition to almost any hot lunch or sandwich.

You can have your po' boy hot or cold, made with anything from fried oysters to bologna. The most famous of Mother's po' boys and one of the Crescent City's definitive sandwiches is known as a Ferdi's Special: ham, beef, debris, and gravy, preferably dressed with pickle slices, lettuce, Creole mustard, and possibly even my'nez, which is how you say "mayonnaise" in New Orleans.

Mother's explains the origin of the Ferdi's Special thus: "Every morning Simon Landry, the original owner, would slice ham and roast beef by hand. One day, Ferdinand 'Ferdi' Stern [no relation to us!] . . . asked Mr. Landry to put some roast beef on his ham po' boy. Or maybe Ferdi wanted some ham on his roast beef po' boy. No one knows." As for the origins of debris, Mother's notes that debris is a word applied to what's left on the ground after a hurricane strikes. "Debris originated when someone asked Mr. Landry, while cutting a roast beef, 'to put some of that debris' on their roast beef po' boy. . . . Thus debris was born." Debris makes this sandwich one of the messiest on earth, so no matter how neat you try to be when you eat it, your table is guaranteed to look like the aftermath of a fraternity food fight.

If you are not running a restaurant, there will likely be only one or two days of the year when making a Ferdi's Special is feasible: after Christmas or Easter or any significant feast time, when it is your job to carve roast beef, ham, and even turkey, so that a lot of crunchy, crusty luscious parts fall to the cutting board to be collected for next-day sandwiches.

Any other time of year, hack up whatever meat you've got—pot roast, chicken, chicken skin, cooked bacon, etc.—and mix the shreds with beef gravy (even store-bought gravy works).

MAKES 2 SANDWICHES

 1 12-inch loaf French bread
 ½ cup debris in gravy (see headnote)
 4 slices baked ham
 4 slices roast beef
   Mayonnaise, Creole mustard or yellow mustard, shredded cabbage, and/or pickles

Slice the French bread in half horizontally and scoop out some of the insides. Use the deeper half to hold the debris. On top of the debris, layer the ham and roast beef. Apply the preferred condiments either to the layer of roast beef or to the other half of the bread, whichever is neater. Moving quickly, bring the two halves together and use a very sharp knife to cut the sandwich into two 6-inch lengths. (Even the sharpest knife will tend to start the inevitable spillage of debris.)

*⁎ Fish Sandwich

In 1980 Joe Coleman, of Wheeling, West Virginia, went to Boston and set sail on a fishing trawler. "I did every job you could do on that boat," he says. "I stood watch, I swabbed the deck, I hauled 'em in and stacked them in the hold. I followed the fish from the water to the pier to the auction. Then I rode in the front seat of the truck that carried the fish back to Wheeling. I trimmed it, I breaded it, I fried it, I made a fish sandwich from it, and I ate it."

We have no doubt that the sandwich Joe Coleman ate that day was delicious. His seafood shop is legendary for the simple perfection of its fish sandwich: two pieces of soft white bread holding a cluster of steaming-hot fillets. The golden crust on the fish is cracker meal, thin as parchment. When you break through it, your sense of smell is tickled by the oceanic perfume, and as the pearl-white fish seeps its luscious flavor, you are tasting a brand-new food, like no other fish sandwich ever created. Ask the opinion of any of the several hundred people who wait in line at Coleman's Fish Market for a sandwich every day; they will agree that this is the best, in a class by itself.

Joe Coleman gave us precise instructions on making a great fish sandwich. His first order of business was to underscore the importance of getting high-quality fillets. "Make sure that the fish fillets are moist, smooth, and have little or no odor," he instructed.

Tartar sauce is necessary.

MAKES 8 SANDWICHES

2 pounds North Atlantic cod, haddock, hake, or pollock fillets
All-purpose flour for dredging
¼ cup Seasoning Mix (recipe follows)
1 large egg
3 cups milk
Fine cracker meal (store-bought or make by pulverizing Saltines)
Canola, sunflower, or soybean oil for deep-frying
16 slices white bread

Cut the fish fillets into 8 equal portions, about ½ inch thick. Place some flour on a plate and dip both sides of the fish fillets into the flour.

Stir the seasoning mix, egg, and milk together in a large, wide bowl. Place the cracker meal in a shallow dish.

Dip the fillets into the egg mixture, then dredge them in the cracker meal.

Pour 3 to 4 inches of oil into a deep fryer or a large deep skillet and heat to 350 degrees. Lower the fillets into the oil, a few at a time, and cook, turning once, until golden brown, 4 to 5 minutes. Drain on paper towels.

Place each fillet between 2 slices of bread. Serve immediately.

Seasoning Mix

MAKES ABOUT 1 CUP

¾ cup salt
¼ cup Accent seasoning
½ tablespoon freshly ground pepper

Combine all the ingredients in a small bowl. Stored in an airtight container, this mix keeps indefinitely.

COLEMAN'S MAGNIFICENT FISH SANDWICH

In the Ohio River Valley between Cincinnati and Pittsburgh, fish sandwiches are as important a part of the nutrition chart as cream pies are in Wisconsin and chili cheese-burgers in New Mexico. In fact, you will find good fish sandwiches throughout the Midwest, where a passion for fried things (pork tenderloin, chicken, cheese curds, corn dogs) combines with the former Catholic prohibition against meat on Fridays as well as a mostly bygone tradition of angling the Great Lakes for pickerel (aka lake jack).

The best known of all the region's fish sandwiches is served in Wheeling, West Virginia, at Coleman's Fish Market, in the city's century-old Centre Market House. During Lent, Coleman's sells ten thousand fish sandwiches in a week, and on Good Friday the line of customers waiting to order one stretches into the street from eight in the morning until after dark. One busy March noontime, we met a delivery boy from a chain pizzeria that promises quick service standing in Coleman's line. He was holding a ready-to-deliver pizza in a thermal tote as he waited to pick up his lunch at Coleman's counter.

"When we are busy, we can do a sandwich every three seconds," Joe Coleman boasts. "Do a sandwich" refers to the final steps in a methodical process that starts with North Atlantic pollock, which, Joe is eager to point out, is different from the Alaskan pollock that fast-food franchises use.

The fish is delivered to a small, quiet cutting room across the street from his self-service restaurant and fish market. In this serene space, which has an appetizing fresh marine fragrance, three or four women spend the day trimming big lengths of the rosy pollock into pieces that are properly sized for frying. You might think that people who cut fillets all day would become blindingly fast at their job and do it with the rote indifference of a widget-twister on an assembly line. The women we watched one afternoon were indeed efficient, gliding their knives through the heavy sides of fish with ease and certainty. And yet we were agog at the degree of focus they applied to the minutiae of the procedure: removing the fat line and each dark spot, speck, and blemish, then partitioning the table-size section of fish to create plump, sandwich-size pieces that were each immaculate. Every fillet is attended with deliberation. Sections of the fish that are a bit too big to be right for the fry basket receive an incision in one side so the cutter can partially butterfly them to the proper thickness before laying them in the pan that holds the readied fillets in rows of precise formation.

From the cutting room, the fish goes to the open kitchen at the back of the market, where it is dredged in flour, dipped in seasoned egg wash, and coated with fine cracker meal, then fried until crisp, during which the shimmering pink meat turns snow-white, its moisture encased in crust. In less time than it will take you to read this sentence, the crunchy fillets are emptied from the fry basket, arranged between two pieces of white bread, wrapped, and delivered to a customer waiting at the counter.

"How is it?" Joe Coleman asks as we take a bite. "Is it sweet? Is it white-white?"

As we nod, he beams, for he is a man with an effervescent pride in the sand-wiches he makes.

"Did it really crunch?" he wants to know. "Did the crust have a clean taste?"

Yes, and yes.

✳ French Dip

PHILIPPE THE ORIGINAL ✳ LOS ANGELES, CALIFORNIA

One day in 1918 a counterman at Philippe's—pronounced Fil-*ee*-peez—was preparing a beef sandwich. The roll fell into a pan of gravy. Fetched out with tongs, the drippings-sopped bread looked so good that an impatient customer said, "I'll take it just like that." That's Philippe's account of the birth of the French dip sandwich: beef on French bread au jus. Whether or not the story is true, Philippe's feels historically correct: a sawdust-on-the-floor hash house from a film noir, where your tablemates range from racetrack touts to SoCal creative types seeking a dose of old-fashioned reality.

Philippe's moved from its original location in 1951 when the freeway was built, but the current restaurant is as comfy as an old shoe: communal tables, dime-a-cup coffee, and fine sandwiches with roaring-hot mustard on the side. Still on the menu are pickled spiced eggs, hard-cooked and displayed at the carving counter in big glass jars of pink beet juice, and pigs' feet. Proprietor John Binder boasted that Philippe's prepares all its feet from scratch and moves at least three hundred pounds of them per week. Philippe's also offers French-dipped lamb and ham.

Philippe's is as good a people-watching place as any snooty spot in Beverly Hills, but instead of movie stars, you see the Angelenos Raymond Carver wrote about—downtowners who include municipal employees from the nearby post office and courthouse as well as Santa Anita touts who frequent the bank of old wooden phone booths, racing forms in hand. Sequestered jurors are sometimes taken to Philippe's upstairs dining room for lunch, and Mr. Binder said that when courtroom tensions run high, the jurors' stress shows in their behavior at the restaurant. "They had real attitudes," he said about one high-profile case whose jurors he served. "They always demanded extra cups of gravy. I said, 'You can't talk to me. You want more gravy, tell your bailiff.'"

The beef, roll, and gravy are all excellent, but in our opinion what puts this sandwich over the top is Philippe's hot mustard. You can use another brand, but for the real deal, we highly recommend getting some of the Original's. It can be ordered at Philippe's Web site (http://stores.yahoo.com/philippes/hotmustard.html) or by phone (213-628-3781).

You cannot order fewer than six jars at a time, but if you are a mustard lover, you'll want to have this on hand for all sorts of sandwiches.

MAKES 1 SANDWICH

1	cup beef stock or canned au jus
1	hard-crusted torpedo roll
3-4	ounces warm roast beef, thinly sliced (enough to pile about 1 inch high in the roll)
	Hot mustard (see headnote)

To make the gravy, pour off the grease from the pan in which you roasted the beef. Place the pan over medium-high heat and pour the beef stock into the pan, stirring to loosen the brown bits. Stir and scrape and bring to a boil. *Voilà.* If you didn't just roast the beef, warm beef stock or canned au jus and use that for dipping.

Slice the roll in half lengthwise. Dip the interior of each half of the roll into the gravy long enough to soften the bread, but not so long that the juice soaks through and softens the crust. Heap in the roast beef and serve with mustard alongside.

✳ Fresser

The world of deli sandwiches is populated by extremists. While most good delis offer nice, simple sandwiches that are made up of normal amounts of one or two ingredients between two slices of bread, it is part of the culture to create sandwiches that are outrageously stuffed with massive amounts of multiple ingredients. These creations grow so tall, and their elements ooze and spill from the bread so readily, that although they still resemble sandwiches to a small degree, they cannot be eaten in any normal way. Even the application of knife and fork is sure to upset the balance, ultimately making for a plate on which all the different ingredients, including the bread, have become a royal hodgepodge.

It is common when ordering such sandwiches to request two or four extra slices of bread, then reapportion the ingredients in such a way that you have several hefty sandwiches made from all the stuff that composed the one. It is also traditional to leave the deli with a doggie bag in which you have that night's midnight snack, and maybe the next day's lunch too.

One of the most awesome such creations is D. Z. Akins's Fresser. From the Yiddish word *fresser,* meaning "one who eats," this architectonic wonder seems to defy the laws of balance when it is brought from the kitchen to your table. There is absolutely no way to savor all its ingredients in a single bite. We recommend serving this one with a whole loaf of rye bread on the side. That way, it is a single sandwich that in fact serves two or three hungry people.

We think it's best to buy all the meats at a good Jewish deli. Few home cooks can replicate the flavors created in the restaurant-size boil pots and steam cabinets.

MAKES 1 SANDWICH

3-4	slices corned beef, warmed
3-4	slices pastrami
3-4	slices roast turkey
3-4	slices rare roast beef
2	slices Swiss cheese
2-3	slices tomato
	Mustard to taste
2	slices rye bread

Pile all the ingredients except the mustard between the slices of bread and use long wooden skewers to hold the sandwich together. Cut it in half with a very sharp knife and pull the halves apart so the striated layers can be seen when the sandwich is served.

Serve with ramekins of mustard for spreading on individual segments of the sandwich.

*✳️ Fried Bologna

G & R TAVERN ✳️ WALDO, OHIO

The fried bologna sandwich used to be a rarity found only in West Virginia, but now it appears on menus as far west as Memphis, Tennessee. It was even a featured attraction at the Gilroy (California) Garlic Festival in 2004. For those who grew up thinking of bologna as a circle of pale pink lunch meat about 1/16 inch thin, it's not such an appetizing concept, but if you actually order one of these sandwiches in a restaurant that takes them seriously, such as the G & R Tavern of Waldo, Ohio, your image of bologna will never again be the same.

In this friendly community tavern, the bologna is sliced thick and is seriously flavorful stuff, a pork and beef blend that is garlic-scented and so fatty that when it sizzles in a skillet, it develops a wickedly savory crust enveloping the moist meat within. G & R loads it into a sandwich with sweet pickles and onion (a great condiment combo) or your choice of mustard, mayonnaise, and/or tomato. Fitting side dishes include a variety of deep-fried vegetables and curly fries.

The primary challenge of making such a sandwich at home is getting bologna worthy of frying. While it is possible to have a supermarket butcher cut thick slices from the national-brand lunch meats, we recommend going the extra mile to get the good stuff. The best ones we've found are "ring bolognas" of a smaller diameter than the familiar sandwich slices. We love Pella (Iowa) bologna, and you won't find a better product than that made by Drier's Meat Market in Michigan, which is set up for mail order (888-521-3999; www.driers.com).

MAKES 1 SANDWICH

4 ounces sliced bologna; either 1 large, thick slice or several smaller slices
2 tablespoons butter
  Sliced Gouda or American cheese (optional)
1 large hard roll or hero roll, cut in half
  Suggested combos of additions: sweet pickle chips and mustard, or sliced
  fresh tomato and mayonnaise

Score the edges of the bologna all around so it doesn't curl up as it cooks. Melt the butter in a skillet and fry the bologna until it is crisp on the outside but still juicy inside, 3 to 4 minutes per side.

As the bologna cooks, prepare the roll: Lay the cheese, if desired, on the bottom of the roll, and dress the top with mayonnaise or mustard to taste.

Pile the hot bologna straight from the skillet into the roll atop the cheese so its heat will soften and melt the cheese. Pile on the additions, if desired, and serve.

Fried Eggs, Bacon, and Gorgonzola

'WICHCRAFT ✳ NEW YORK, NEW YORK

The name 'Wichcraft isn't only a play on the word "sandwich." It's a nod to the craft of cooking. Chef Sisha Ortuzar was previously sous-chef at Gramercy Tavern, whose chef-owner, Tom Colicchio, opened the well-respected Craft steak house on 19th Street in 2002. Shortly after that, when a space next to Craft became available, Sisha moved in and opened a restaurant devoted exclusively to sandwiches, naming it with a bow to his partner, Colicchio. There are now several locations in New York.

"In general, sandwiches are not done well," Sisha told us. "In part, that is because many people have this feeling, 'It's just a sandwich.' I beg to differ. A sandwich has all the potential to be something special."

While the menu at Sisha's sandwich-focused restaurant includes many exotic and far-flung concepts, the fried egg sandwich is as familiar as can be. But it is made special by a few twists on the bacon-egg-cheese formula that is available in every corner deli, as well as by the use of the very best components. The combination of Gorgonzola and four-star bacon elevates the everyday breakfast combo into luxury class, making this a sandwich every bit as right for a late-night candlelit supper as for the rooster patrol.

Nieman Ranch doesn't handle mail-order, but we can usually find the bacon at our local Trader Joe's.

MAKES 4 SANDWICHES

4	ciabatta rolls or other crusty, light rolls
4	ounces Gorgonzola dolce, cut into 4 equal pieces
12	thick slices Nieman Ranch bacon, cooked until crisp (see headnote)
4	ounces frisée lettuce, coarsely chopped (about 1½ cups)
	Olive oil
	Red wine vinegar
	Kosher salt and freshly ground pepper
	Butter
8	large eggs

Slice each roll in half and spread the Gorgonzola over the top halves. Place 3 strips of bacon on each bottom half. Then toast all the halves in a toaster oven or a very hot oven (450 degrees) only until the cheese softens.

Put the frisée in a medium bowl and toss it with a little olive oil, red wine vinegar, and salt and pepper to taste.

Melt some butter in a large skillet and fry the eggs to "over medium," seasoning them to taste with salt and pepper. Place 2 fried eggs on the bottom half of each roll and top them off with the frisée. Place the top half of the rolls on the frisée and serve.

*⁎⁎ Fried Flounder

Frying is an art in the Lowcountry, and nowhere is it done more deliciously than at the Old Post Office, a restaurant that is at once local and worldly, down-home and daring.

"This is the best fried fish sandwich out there," declares chef Philip Bardin. There are two reasons fish sandwiches hereabouts are extraordinary. First, the pieces of fish used are huge. Indeed, we have been to some restaurants in which the "flounder sandwich" is only nominally a sandwich. Really it's two pitifully small-looking pieces of bread on either side of a gigantic crisp-fried fillet. You do eat it like a sandwich, and the bread is most helpful in getting the fish to your mouth, but in such cases the taste of the bread is inconsequential. The second reason South Carolina flounder sandwiches are special is the flounder itself. The flounder you find in restaurants along the mid-Atlantic coast, from the Chesapeake Bay to Savannah, is whiter, creamier, and sweeter-fleshed than the fish that is called flounder everywhere else. It seems like a whole different species.

Most of the Carolina flounder sandwiches we've had have been very basic. As mentioned, they come on plain bread, and the only available condiment is tartar sauce. Chef Bardin transcends that by adding sweet Vidalia onion slices and artichoke relish, creating a tartar sauce with vegetable verve. The result is nothing short of spectacular. Note that you need to make the tartar sauce well in advance.

MAKES 2 SANDWICHES

1 cup buttermilk

2 large eggs, beaten

Kosher salt

1 large flounder fillet (at least 12 ounces), cut in half

2 cups peanut oil

1 cup all-purpose flour, mixed with 1 cup fine cracker crumbs or meal

Fresh lemon juice

1 Vidalia onion, sliced into thin rings

Olive oil

Freshly ground pepper

4 slices top-quality rye bread

2 large leaves Bibb or Boston lettuce

Artichoke Tartar Sauce (recipe follows)

Mix the buttermilk, eggs, and 1 tablespoon kosher salt in a wide, shallow bowl. Soak the flounder fillet halves in this mixture for 20 minutes.

Heat the peanut oil in a large skillet until very hot (at least 400 degrees).

Place the flour mixture in another wide, shallow bowl. Remove the flounder from the buttermilk mixture and dredge it in the flour mixture.

Fry the flounder in the hot oil, turning it once, for about 3 minutes per side. Remove when just done, sprinkle with lemon juice, and set aside.

Brush the Vidalia onion slices with a bit of olive oil and sprinkle them with salt and pepper to taste. In a separate skillet, or better yet on a countertop grill, cook the onion slices until tender. Set them aside.

Toast the rye bread in the same skillet after removing the onion.

Place a lettuce leaf on 1 piece of bread. Top with a cooked flounder fillet and then some of the onion slices. Let stand for at least 3 minutes for the flavors to marry. Spread half of the artichoke tartar sauce on the top piece of bread, place the top piece on the sandwich, and slice in half. Repeat with the remaining bread, lettuce, fish, onion slices, and tartar sauce to make another sandwich.

✻✻ Artichoke Tartar Sauce

Artichoke relish is available in many gourmet food stores, and there is nothing better alongside porky butter beans. Artichoke relish can be mail-ordered from Carolina FoodPros (877-728-2783; www.carolinafoodpros.com).

MAKES ABOUT ¾ CUP

- ½ cup mayonnaise
- 1 tablespoon fresh lemon juice
  Dash of Tabasco sauce
- 2 tablespoons artichoke relish

Combine all the ingredients in a small bowl and stir. Cover and refrigerate for at least 6 hours or overnight.

ROASTING PEPPERS

One of the nicest complements for almost any sandwich made of oink or moo or only vegetables is a layer of roasted peppers — either sweet bell peppers, which can be red, yellow, green, or orange, or hotter chile peppers. While many stores sell jars of them already roasted, it's easy to do it yourself. And home-roasted peppers have a toothy bite that jarred ones seldom retain.

Few foods smell as distinctive as roasting chile pepper pods. Earthy and pungent, roasted peppers are, in fact, a favorite roadside snack during harvesttime in New Mexico: fresh out of the roaster, they are stemmed, seeded, and sandwiched between slabs of rough-grained bread or inside a tortilla to make a delicious sandwich.

The best way to prepare them is to roast the peppers directly under a hot broiler or over a flame. You must be absolutely vigilant as you do this, for the goal is to blacken the skin but not burn the flesh. Therefore the roasting peppers need to be tended constantly and turned as they cook so they blacken evenly. Once they are blackened, remove them from their proximity to the flame and wrap each pepper in a damp paper towel for a few minutes. This will quicken their cooling so they can be handled, and it will help you to peel off the skin. The skin should strip away easily. Once they are peeled, it is best *not* to wash the peppers, as you will wash away some of their flavor. Split them open and remove the stem and seeds, and they are ready to be piled into a sandwich or served alongside one.

NOTE: If the peppers you are roasting, peeling, and seeding have any heat whatsoever, *wear gloves when handling them* to avoid getting fiery chile oil on your fingers. The oil is difficult to remove, and it is hell if you happen to scratch anywhere near your eyes with some of it still on your fingers. You can ignore this warning only when you handle mild bell peppers.

Fry Bread Open-Face

LEONA'S ✳ CHIMAYO, NEW MEXICO

Fry bread is popular throughout the American Southwest, where Native American cooks use it as the foundation for breakfast, lunch, and supper. A close cousin to the New Mexican sopapilla, fry bread is sometimes served just plain, with honey on the side or dusted with cinnamon, and it is the bottom layer of what's known in the region as an Indian taco—all the ingredients that are normally folded into a tortilla heaped atop a round of bread.

Leona Medina Tiede, of Chimayo, New Mexico, suggests that fry bread is good when split open and stuffed with meat, beans, and/or cheese. In her delightful little cookbook, *Leona's Sanctuary,* she offers the recipe for making good fry bread along with the recipe for this great open-face vegetarian sandwich.

MAKES 6 OPEN-FACE SANDWICHES

DOUGH

2	cups all-purpose flour
1/3	cup dry powdered milk
2 1/2	teaspoons baking powder
1/2	teaspoon salt
3	tablespoons shortening
2/3–3/4	cup lukewarm water
	Vegetable oil for frying

FILLING

2	cups cooked pinto beans or black beans
2	cups chopped mixed crisp salad greens
30	cherry tomatoes, cut in half
1 1/2	cups roasted corn kernels (available at Trader Joe's, or see recipe opposite)
1 1/2	cups roasted chile pepper strips (see page 89)
	Optional additions: chopped scallions, avocado chunks, shredded cheese, and/or chopped fresh oregano

PREPARE THE DOUGH: Stir together the flour, powdered milk, baking powder, and salt in a large bowl. Cut in the shortening with your fingers or two knives until the mixture has the consistency of pea-size crumbs. Stir in the water a little at a time, using only enough for the mixture to form a ball.

Turn the dough onto a lightly floured board and knead until it is soft and no longer sticky, 3 to 4 minutes. Divide it into 6 equal portions, cover them with a damp kitchen towel, and let stand for 1 hour.

Shape the dough into six ½-inch-thick rounds. Pat or roll each round out on a floured board to form a disk 6 to 7 inches in diameter. Poke a hole through the center with your finger.

FRY THE DOUGH: In a heavy skillet, heat 1 inch of oil to 365 degrees. Gently slip a dough round into the oil. Fry it for 2 minutes, flip, and fry the other side until it is golden brown and puffy. Remove the fry bread from the oil with a slotted spoon and drain it on paper towels. Repeat with the remaining dough rounds.

ASSEMBLE THE SANDWICHES: Let the fry bread sit until just barely warm. Spread the bread with the beans, salad greens, tomatoes, corn kernels, chile pepper strips, and other ingredients to taste. Serve immediately.

Roasted Corn

Preheat a barbecue grill. Remove the outer husk of an ear of corn. Pull down the inner husks and remove as much of the silk as possible. Replace the inner husks to encase the cob thoroughly. Roast over hot coals, turning it occasionally, for 10 to 12 minutes. The husks will brown but the kernels underneath should not char. Remove the cob from the fire, pull away the husks, and use a sharp knife to shave the kernels off the corn. (Each cob should yield about ⅓ cup.)

✳✳ Garden Egg Salad

DUTCH KITCHEN ✳✳ FRACKVILLE, PENNSYLVANIA

What's a sandwich book without egg salad? But a recipe that calls for chopped egg and mayonnaise isn't all that interesting. To the rescue comes the Dutch Kitchen of Frackville, Pennsylvania, where egg salad is just one of many salads that are suitable not only for sandwiches but for a dinner buffet.

In Pennsylvania Dutch country, the array of good things to eat on that table is known as "seven sweets and seven sours," a tradition that goes back to the need to can, pickle, and cure in order to preserve the garden's yield throughout the year. Historians don't know if it ever really was a custom to put exactly seven sweet things and seven sour ones on the dinner table, but some believe that the ritual in guesthouses was for guests to count and merrily reprimand a hostess whose total didn't add up to fourteen.

Today at the Dutch Kitchen, there are far more than fourteen items on the salad bar, and among them is this garden-freshened version of the lunch-counter classic. The carrot, pepper, and onion balance the smoothness of the eggs. It's good on a bed of lettuce with tomatoes on the side, and great on toast or bread.

MAKES 4 SANDWICHES

5 eggs, hard-cooked (see page 45)
³/₄ cup mayonnaise
¼ teaspoon salt
¼ teaspoon freshly ground pepper
2 tablespoons finely chopped carrot
2 tablespoons finely chopped green bell pepper
1 tablespoon diced red onion
8 slices bread or toast
    Sweet pickles for serving

Peel and dice the eggs and place them in a medium bowl. Add all the other ingredients except the bread and pickles. Mix well, but don't mix so much that the eggs are pulverized.

Spread the egg salad on 4 slices of bread or toast, top with the remaining slices, and serve with sweet pickles on the side.

Green Tomato BLT

Of all the variations on the classic theme of the BLT, the Loveless Cafe's version, layered with crisp fried green tomatoes, is one of the most beguiling. The tang of the tomatoes and their brittle crunch provide extraordinary balance for the savor of bacon and the gentle notes of mayo and lettuce.

This BLT is a recent addition to the menu, part of a kitchen expansion program that went into place after the mid-twentieth-century café was bought by one of its biggest fans, Nashville native Tom Morales. Tom has made a name for himself as one of the premier caterers to the movie business, and when he heard that the Loveless was for sale, he heard the old place calling his name. He recalled coming to the café as a child for family-style meals of fried chicken, ham, biscuits, gravy, and homemade peach and blackberry preserves, and the thought that this beloved culinary legacy might be lost if it were sold to the wrong person—or, worse yet, replaced by some fast-food franchise—made him realize that he needed to shepherd it into the twenty-first century.

While Tom has modernized the kitchen and expanded the menu to include the likes of this remarkable sandwich (as well as smoked-there barbecue), the mainstays remain. That means not only chicken and ham and biscuits but much of the staff of cooks and waitresses who make dining in this good place such a pleasure for anyone searching for a true taste of the South.

MAKES 1 SANDWICH

3-4	slices green tomato
	Salt and freshly ground pepper
1	cup yellow cornmeal
1	cup canola oil
3	tablespoons mayonnaise
2	slices wheatberry bread, toasted
2-3	lettuce leaves
3-4	thick bacon strips, cooked

Season the sliced tomatoes with salt and pepper and dredge them in the cornmeal.

Heat the canola oil in a skillet to 350 degrees. Fry the tomatoes for 4 to 5 minutes, or until crisp and golden brown on both sides. Remove from the oil and drain on paper towels.

Spread the mayonnaise on the toast. Place lettuce on both sides of the toast. Place the fried green tomatoes and bacon on 1 piece of the toast. Put the top on the sandwich and cut in half. Serve.

Grilled Gruyère with Braised Leeks on Multigrain Bread

CLEMENTINE ✳✳ LOS ANGELES, CALIFORNIA

If you like sunshiny food, you'll love Clementine. A small, personable bakery that makes everything from scratch every day, it features a delectable array of breakfast pastries, cupcakes, and cookies and a lunch menu of sandwiches, seasonal salads, and soups made from ingredients bought at local farmers' markets. You can dine here, and everything is available to take home and eat. In addition, Clementine specializes in magnificent gift baskets that include the likes of a Valentine's Day assortment featuring heart-shaped brownies and an all-purpose Sweet Treat Basket with cookies, brownies, homemade caramels, and citrus candies.

The heart and soul behind Clementine is Annie Milar, a Minnesotan who trained at the Cordon Bleu in London and has worked at some of the most esteemed restaurants in Los Angeles, including Campanile, Spago Beverly Hills, and La Brea Bakery. She says, "I wanted to take what I learned about cooking from my mom and my grandma, combine it with my restaurant experience, and offer something unique and homemade to the neighborhood." And when we told her about this book and asked her to explain what her goal was at Clementine, Annie said, "My mission in life is to bring a small bit of comfort and pleasure to the people in our community—and melted cheese served by friendly people is one of the best ways I know to do that. Banana cream pie made with homemade graham crackers is another good way!"

MAKES 4 SANDWICHES

BRAISED LEEKS

2	medium leeks
¼	cup extra-virgin olive oil
½	cup water
	Grated zest and juice of ½ lemon
1	teaspoon fresh thyme leaves
	Scant ½ teaspoon salt
	Pinch of freshly ground pepper
	Butter for spreading
8	slices dense multigrain bread
10	ounces Gruyère cheese, thinly sliced
	Dijon mustard

BRAISE THE LEEKS: Preheat the oven to 400 degrees.

Trim off the root end of the leeks. Slice them lengthwise and remove any tough, dark green portions by cutting away from the root end on an angle and peeling them off. Clean the leeks thoroughly under running water to remove any dirt. Pat dry.

Heat a large skillet and add 2 tablespoons of the olive oil. When the oil is hot, carefully place the leeks in the pan, cut side down. Cook for a few minutes, just until they are golden brown on one side. Remove the leeks and arrange them cut side up in a casserole dish. Add the water, lemon juice, and remaining 2 tablespoons olive oil. Sprinkle the lemon zest, thyme, salt, and pepper over the top. Cover tightly with aluminum foil and place in the oven.

Bake for 20 to 25 minutes. Then remove the foil and bake uncovered for another 20 minutes. The liquid will reduce and the leeks will caramelize. Let them cool. (The leeks can be braised up to 2 days ahead, covered, and refrigerated.)

TO ASSEMBLE THE SANDWICHES: Thoroughly butter 1 side of each slice of bread and arrange the slices butter side down. Divide the cheese evenly among the bread slices. Cut the braised leeks diagonally into 2-inch lengths and arrange them on 4 of the cheese-topped slices of bread. On each of the other 4 slices, spread about 1 tablespoon Dijon mustard over the cheese (use more or less according to your taste and the strength of your mustard). Place the 2 slices together to make each sandwich. (The sandwiches can be assembled up to 1 day ahead and refrigerated, wrapped tightly in plastic.)

Place a batch of sandwiches in a large skillet over low heat. When they are brown and crispy on one side, flip them over and cook until brown and crispy on the other side, about 10 minutes per side. Keep warm in the oven while you cook the remaining sandwiches. Cut in half and serve.

*⁎⁎ Gyro

CHICAGO, ILLINOIS *⁎⁎

Italian beef and red hots are Chicago's most famous street foods, but the gyro is nearly as popular. In the windows and behind the counters of countless snack shacks are big cylinders of compressed beef and lamb that came to be known as gyros because the cylinders rotate (like a gyroscope)—partly for show, but also because most setups have heat lamps that keep the surface of the cylinder hot.

When you order a gyro (pronounced *yee*-roh), the counterman slices off strips of the meat and heaps them onto a thick circle of pita bread. Onto the meat goes ultra-garlicky tzatziki sauce, then an abundance of shredded lettuce and chopped tomato. Gyros usually are served well wrapped in foil, which helps keep the tubular sandwich intact while you plow into it.

It is our belief that the key element of a great gyro is freshly cooked meat (as opposed to meat cut off a cylinder that's been rotating who knows how long), and the best way to ensure freshness is to make your own meat loaf. It's not something you'll likely want to do for a spur-of-the-moment lunch (the meat loaf needs to be refrigerated overnight), but a nice big loaf of freshly made gyro meat is a grand foundation for a party. Lay out the loaf, the pitas, the tzatziki, and the garnishes, and guests can assemble their own. The meat can also be served sliced on a plate with mashed potatoes on the side (and, of course, a knife and fork).

MAKES 8 LARGE GYROS

Gyro Loaf (recipe follows)
8 large pita breads, heated on a griddle or in the oven, loosely wrapped in foil
Tzatziki Sauce (page 215)
Shredded lettuce
Chopped tomato

Cut about 8 thin slices off the gyro loaf and lay each across the center of a warm pita. Top the meat with some tzatziki sauce, then lettuce and tomato. Roll the bread around the ingredients and use long toothpicks if necessary to keep it rolled. (Alternatively, serve the tzatziki sauce in ramekins on the side for dipping the sandwiches, bite by bite.) Repeat with the remaining pitas.

Gyro Loaf

MAKES ENOUGH FOR 8 GYROS

1½	pounds boneless lamb shoulder, cut into 1- to 2-inch chunks
1	pound boneless chuck roast, cut into 1- to 2-inch chunks
1	tablespoon dried oregano
1	tablespoon salt
1	tablespoon freshly ground pepper
1	teaspoon ground cumin
½	teaspoon cayenne pepper
½	teaspoon ground cinnamon
¼	teaspoon freshly grated nutmeg
¼	teaspoon ground allspice
3–4	garlic cloves, finely minced
1	tablespoon vegetable oil
⅓	cup finely minced onion
10	strips bacon

Combine the lamb and beef in a meat grinder and grind to a fine consistency. (A food processor works, but easy does it. Do not pulverize the meat.) Place the ground meat in a large bowl. In a small bowl, combine the oregano, salt, all the spices, and the garlic, oil, and onion. Add to the meat and mix thoroughly. Cover and refrigerate for 2 hours.

Preheat the oven to 375 degrees.

Simmer the bacon in water for 2 to 3 minutes, just long enough to blanch it. Drain on paper towels.

Use the bacon to line the sides and bottom of an 8½-x-5-x-3-inch loaf pan, setting aside 2 or 3 strips. Put the meat mixture in the pan, pressing it in firmly. Top with the remaining bacon strips.

Place the loaf pan in a larger baking pan and pour in enough boiling water to reach halfway up the sides of the loaf pan. Bake for 30 minutes. Reduce the heat to 325 degrees and bake until the meat is firm, another 30 minutes.

Remove the pan from the oven and from its hot water bath. Drain off any excess liquid. Cover the loaf with aluminum foil and place a weight (a brick, for instance) on the foil to compress the meat loaf as much as possible. Set the meat loaf aside to cool.

When the meat loaf is at room temperature (after about 1 hour), refrigerate it, still weighted down, for 8 to 10 hours, or overnight.

When you are ready to make the sandwiches, remove the meat loaf from the refrigerator and let it come to room temperature.

Ham and Cheese Double-Decker

CAMP WASHINGTON CHILI PARLOR ✳ CINCINNATI, OHIO

A bare description of the double-decker makes it seem ordinary, for the ingredient choices are nothing special; they range from bacon and egg to turkey and beef. Any combination is possible, including turkey and turkey, beef and beef, etc., meaning the sandwich is simply a double lode of one favorite ingredient, generally piled in with lettuce, tomato, mayo, mustard, pickle, and so on. What makes Cincinnati's double-decker sandwiches extraordinary is the amount of ingredients they contain and the tidiness of the presentation. No matter how tall, there is no leakage; and experienced sandwich eaters can devour one without dropping so much as a bread crumb. This is a case of the sandwich maker's art being simple, and of simplicity demanding the finest art.

We are especially fond of double-deckers containing hot ham, which is sliced ultra-thin and fitted into the bread in moist clumps, and generally paired with American cheese.

The best place in town to eat double-deckers is Camp Washington Chili Parlor, source of twenty-four-hour-per-day good cheap eats for more than half a century. The proprietor is John Johnson, who started working here for his uncles when he arrived in America from Greece in 1951. John bought the place in 1977, and five years ago moved it across the street to spanking-new quarters, where it remains the gold standard—for breakfast, lunch, dinner, and midnight snacks.

MAKES 1 SANDWICH

3   slices sturdy white bread ("toasting-style" preferred)
    Butter for spreading
    Lettuce leaves
3   ounces baked ham, very thinly sliced (a 1-inch pile)
    Tomato slices
    Mayonnaise to taste
    Mustard to taste (optional)
4   slices American cheese or Velveeta
    Pickle chips

Lightly toast the bread. Butter 2 slices of toast. Lay the lettuce leaves on 1 buttered slice, then pile on the ham, using your hands to compress it into a neat pile that does not extend beyond the crust. Place the tomato slices on top of the ham. Spread mayonnaise on one side of the unbuttered piece of toast and place it, mayo side down, on the tomatoes. If you like mustard, spread it on the top of this slice. Place the cheese on top, and cap the sandwich with the third piece of toast, buttered side down. Use two long toothpicks to hold the sandwich together, and with a very sharp knife, cut it into 2 triangles. Serve with the pickle chips alongside.

UNFASHIONABLE PROCESSED CHEESE

There are few things more delicious in the world than some of the handcrafted cheeses of France and Italy, and of America too — from California chèvre to Iowa blue to Vermont cheddar. Artisanal cheeses have become immensely popular in food-savvy homes and upscale restaurants, but when making sandwiches, they aren't always the right thing to use. They can be hard to slice neatly and impossible to spread on a piece of bread. When melted in a hot sandwich, they may clump or curdle.

Processed cheese solves all the problems. It melts under a broiler as smooth as liquid mercury. It spreads on bread like warm grout. It is a supreme icon of American gastrotechnology: a natural product made supernatural by the addition of emulsifying salts, gums, sweeteners, and flavoring agents, all heated and mixed to a state of exquisite uniformity and stability. Processed cheese comes in a perfectly rectangular brick or in a clear glass jar, in spray cans, or as individually wrapped slices. If you don't have some in your cupboard and refrigerator, well, you're probably a Communist, or worse.

"The archetypal plastic food" is how Warren J. Belasco condemned the stuff in his book *Appetite for Change.* We certainly hope that Professor Belasco never invites us to his house for bologna sandwiches, because we like ours with a nice, shiny slice of Velveeta on top.

"It comes in as many flavors as Jell-O," griped John and Karen Hess about processed cheese in their muckraking *Taste of America,* describing it as "bland and characterless . . . a compound of milk solids and lots of water and chemicals, synthetically flavored . . . sold, often presliced, in airless packages." Most cultural elitists decry any food with a big-corporation taint. But such disrespect is their loss, for they will never know the joy of such red-white-and-blue comfort sandwiches as grilled cheese and bacon on Wonder Bread, which virtually demands flawless factory-made slices of cheese as bright orange as a school bus.

Although processed cheese may seem like a product of the convenience-crazed years after World War II, it actually goes back to 1916, when James Kraft patented a method for blending and pasteurizing cheese to retard spoilage. U.S. troops in World War I ate tons of it, and in the 1920s Kraft enjoyed huge success selling 5-pound bricks of processed cheese to American consumers. It was an idea whose time had come. Popular wisdom in the era between the wars decreed that good health demanded enormous ingestion of protein, vitamins, and minerals. Cheese provided those things aplenty, but for many Americans — particularly those with recent immigrant roots who wanted to assimilate into the culture at large — cheese that smelled bad or had quirky Old World texture was a telltale sign, as shameful as garlic, of outsider status. Processed cheese had no such foreign stigma. Kraft offered bricks of Gruyère that melted more easily than the real stuff, "old English" that had the "tingle on the tongue" flavor of cheddar but was as spreadable as cream cheese, Limburger with "old-time flavor" but no rind or odor, and the crowning glory of the line, still a staple in kitchens coast to coast, Velveeta. Called "cheese food" instead of mere cheese because it was made by mixing cheddar with whey concentrate and milk solids, Velveeta was available in 1-pound bricks with or without pimientos added. In its brick form, which was so easy to slice or melt, Velveeta was a natural for use in sandwiches and casseroles of all kinds; some of Kraft's suggestions in the early years were macaroni and Velveeta, Velveeta pudding, halibut à la Kraft, and Velveeta-stuffed prunes.

On the time line of important moments in sandwich history, 1947 is a banner year, for that is when Kraft first marketed "Singles" — presliced tiles of cheese perfectly sized for sandwiches made on perfectly square slices of bread. For the modern parent too busy to slice cheese to fit lunch-box sandwiches before sending the kids off to school, Singles were a godsend. In her book *I'm a Spam Fan,* Carolyn Wyman reports that consumers at first resisted the idea because the already-sliced cheese was stuck together in such a uniform rectangle that it looked like a solid block. Once store managers learned to open a package and fan out the slices, proving that they peeled away from the block as easily as the top disk off an Oreo, the super-convenient product sold like hotcakes. Eighteen years later, the idea was improved when Kraft began selling packages of slices that were each individually wrapped, thus allowing for indefinite storage even when a package has been opened. If you have some in the refrigerator and any kind of bread in the bread box and a jar of mustard or mayo, you can have a pretty nice sandwich for lunch.

✳ Ham and Pear Crisp

Hell's Kitchen offers far more enticing things to eat than can be sampled at any one meal—
or ten. We won't even try to describe such breakfast triumphs as lemon-ricotta hotcakes and
Mahnomin porridge (based on Native American recipes and using native wild rice). Let's go
right to the sandwiches, of which there are two must-eats. One is a WBLT, which is like a
regular BLT but made with Nueske's applewood-smoked bacon (the best brand there is)
and a couple of cornmeal-dusted walleye pike fillets. Instead of mayo, it is dressed with
lemon-scallion tartar sauce. The other is a ham and pear crisp on sourdough spread
with spiced butter. Chef Mitch Omer shared his recipe for the latter with us.

MAKES 4 SANDWICHES

1	small can (15 ounces) sliced pears in syrup
8	large slices sourdough bread
	Spiced Butter (recipe follows)
4	slices (6 ounces) Swiss cheese
1¼	pounds shaved ham
4	slices (6 ounces) Fontina cheese

Drain the sliced pears in a small strainer. Slice the pears into thin slivers and set aside.

Lay out the 8 slices sourdough bread and spread each with a thin layer of the spiced butter,
using only about half the butter. On each of 4 slices, place 1 slice of Swiss cheese and about a
½-inch pile of shaved ham. Divide the sliced pears among the 4 sandwiches and top each with
a slice of the Fontina cheese. Place the remaining slices of sourdough on top, and press together
gently to compress the sandwiches.

Spread the remaining spiced butter on the outside of the sourdough bread.

Heat a large, heavy skillet over medium-high heat. Place the sandwiches in the skillet, in batches if necessary, and cook for approximately 7 minutes, or until brown and crisp. Using a spatula, turn the sandwiches over and cook for another 7 minutes.

For ease of eating, cut each sandwich in half on the diagonal.

Spiced Butter

MAKES ½ CUP

- 8 ounces (2 sticks) unsalted butter, softened
- 2 teaspoons pumpkin pie spice
- 1 teaspoon ground coriander
- 1 teaspoon ground ginger
- 1 teaspoon kosher salt

Combine the butter and the spices in a small bowl and whisk them together until smooth and evenly incorporated.

Ham Biscuits

Jack Howard started in the biscuit business in 1962, when he opened a small eat-shack in an industrial section of Atlanta. Named for a skillful cook he then employed (she was able to fry 60 dozen eggs in a morning), Mamie's Kitchen has since expanded to four locations east of the city. "In the early days, I used to go to the mountains and buy big cakes of butter from the farmers," Jack recalled. "I bought jars of preserves they made and put them on my tables. My slogan was 'I am rolling in dough.'"

When we asked Jack to explain why his biscuits are so good, he said, "We don't roll them with a rolling pin; we don't cut them with a can; we don't make them from a recipe." He lifted a hot one off its paper plate and cupped it in one hand, using a deft twist of his other hand to separate its top and raise it like a Tiffany salesman showing what's inside a ring box. A buttermilk-scented cloud of steam wafted up. "This is what you call a 'scratch biscuit,'" he continued. "It is made from nothing but White Lily flour, buttermilk, and lard. Pure, refined lard," he emphasized. "Enough of each goes into a big bowl where your biscuit maker kneads the dough, but not too much. She knows when to pull one off, pat it out, and put it in the pan." Between fifteen hundred and two thousand biscuits are made this way six days a week, from before the doors open at 5:30 A.M. until closing time at 2 P.M.

Any time you order a biscuit, it comes hot from the oven. Its knobby golden surface has a gentle crunch, and although the inside is fleecy, it is not fragile. While it is delicious plain or simply buttered, its best destiny is to be pulled into two round, gold-topped halves so it can sandwich a slice or two of deliriously flavorful country ham grilled until its rim of fat becomes translucent amber and the brick-red surface starts to turn crisp. The power of the ham—its complexity, its salty punch, its rugged, chewy texture—is perfectly complemented by the fluffy gentleness of the biscuit around it.

If plain grilled country ham packs too much of a wallop (and it does for many), cushion the flavor slightly by using the ham mix formula we got many years ago from Helen Dickerson, who was chef at the old Chalfonte Hotel in Cape May, New Jersey.

FLOUR NOTE: Many southern biscuit makers swear by White Lily brand, which has slightly less protein than most brands. If you can't get it, use 1 cup cake flour and 1 cup unbleached all-purpose flour. Do *not* use self-rising flour.

MAKES 8 TO 10 BISCUITS

BISCUITS

2	cups flour (see above)
1	tablespoon baking powder
½	teaspoon salt
¼	cup cold lard, cut into sugar-cube size (or, if the food police are watching, use a half-and-half mix of solid vegetable shortening and butter)
1	cup cold buttermilk

HAM MIX

10-12	ounces country ham
⅓	cup mayonnaise

PREPARE THE BISCUITS: Preheat the oven to 500 degrees.

Place the flour, baking powder, and salt in a large bowl. Using two knives or a pastry cutter, cut the lard into the mixture until it resembles a coarse meal. Stir in the buttermilk. Do not overmix! (You can mix this in a food processor using two to three pulses, but beware: overmixing equals tough biscuits.) Separate the dough into 8 to 10 plum-size pieces. Using your hands as gently as possible, shape them into slightly flattened rounds. Place the rounds on a cookie sheet and bake for 8 to 10 minutes, until the tops are light golden brown. Cool slightly.

MEANWHILE, MAKE THE HAM MIX: Chop the country ham into tiny pieces. Mix with the mayonnaise.

Never slice a biscuit. Using both hands, gingerly twist the top from the bottom. Spoon the ham mix onto the bottom, place the other half on top, and serve warm.

✳✳ Hoosier Reuben

SHAPIRO'S DELI ✳✳ INDIANAPOLIS, INDIANA

Here's a story—amazing, but true. After several months of going to some of New York's best kosher-style delicatessens and getting sandwiches of good cold cuts and/or cured meats on mediocre rye bread (spongy, soft-crusted, lightweight), we took a trip to Indianapolis, Indiana, and finally found the deli sandwich of our dreams, made on first-rate rye. This might seem a little odd, because Indianapolis is not generally known as a source of great Jewish food, but anyone who has been to Shapiro's Delicatessen knows the truth: here is some of the best Jewish food there is, anywhere in the U.S.A. Not just sandwiches, either. You can have corned beef omelets, matzo ball soup, potato pancakes, and babkas, too. But it's the sandwiches on rye we like the best.

So we asked Brian Shapiro how to make a Reuben, which is in some ways the quintessential Jewish deli sandwich. Brian explained that there are two basic kinds of Reubens: the regular style, made with warm sauerkraut, and the New York style, in which creamy coleslaw is substituted for the sauerkraut. (And there is the Reuben's parallel sandwich, the Rachel, made with pastrami instead of corned beef.)

According to Craig Claiborne's *New York Times Food Encyclopedia,* the Reuben was invented at Reuben's Restaurant in New York. He quotes Patricia B. Taylor, daughter of Arnold Reuben, founder of the restaurant, describing its genesis thus:

The year was 1914. Late one evening a leading lady of actor Charlie Chaplin's came into the restaurant and said, "Reuben, make me a sandwich, make it a combination, I'm so hungry I could eat a brick." He took a loaf of rye bread, cut two slices on the bias and stacked one piece with sliced Virginia ham, roast turkey, and imported Swiss cheese, topped off with coleslaw and lots of Reuben's special Russian dressing and the second slice of bread. . . . He served it to the lady who said, "Gee, Reuben, this is the best sandwich I ever ate, you ought to call it an Annette Seelos Special." To which he replied, "Like hell I will, I'll call it a Reuben's Special."

Over the years, corned beef has replaced the ham and turkey, but the configuration of meat, dressing, and slaw has remained the basic definition.

MAKES 2 SANDWICHES

10 slices corned beef from a good deli, warmed
4 large, thick slices rye bread, preferably bakery-fresh
¼ cup sauerkraut, warmed, or cool creamy coleslaw
4 slices Emmenthaler Swiss cheese
2 tablespoons store-bought Thousand Island dressing
Butter or margarine for grilling

Layer 5 slices of the corned beef on each of 2 slices of the rye bread. Top each with half of the sauerkraut or coleslaw. Next add 2 slices of Swiss cheese to each. Finally spread the dressing over the Swiss cheese and close the sandwiches.

Heat some butter or margarine in a heavy skillet over medium heat. Set the sandwiches in the pan and cook until the exterior of the bread is well browned. Flip the sandwiches over and toast the other side. Cut in half and serve.

✳ Hoosier Tenderloin

NICK'S KITCHEN ✳ **HUNTINGTON, INDIANA**

Historians believe the Midwest tenderloin was first served to the public just west of Fort Wayne, Indiana, in the town of Huntington (home of former vice president Dan Quayle). Nick Frienstein started frying breaded pork cutlets in 1904, to sell in sandwiches from a street cart in town; four years later he opened Nick's Kitchen. The method of preparation changed one winter shortly after Nick opened the café, when Nick's brother Jake suffered such severe frostbite that he lost all his fingers. Jake, whose job it had been to bread the slices of pork, found that his stumps made good tools for pounding the meat to make it tender. Since then, nearly all the Midwest's tenderloins have been either beaten tender (with a wooden hammer) or run through a mechanical tenderizer (or both).

Now run by Jean Anne Bailey, whose father bought the café in 1969, Nick's Kitchen lists its tenderloin on the menu with a challenge that's ironic, considering its culinary history: "Bet You Need Both Hands." In fact, two hands are barely adequate for hoisting this colossal sandwich, which is built around a wavy disk of audibly crunchy pork that extends a good 2 to 3 inches beyond the circumference of a 5-inch bun, virtually eclipsing its plate. Soaked in buttermilk, which gives a tangy twist to the meat's sweetness, and tightly encased in a coat of rugged cracker crumbs (not the more typical finely ground cracker meal), the lode of pork inside the crust fairly drips with moisture. Jean Anne told us she buys the meat already cut and cubed. She pounds it, marinates it, breads it, and fries it.

(We must offer a parenthesis to alert you to Jean Anne's pies. "My father served frozen ones," she says. "I knew I wanted something better." Made using a hand-me-down dough recipe that incorporates a bit of corn syrup, her fruit pies have a flaky crust that evaporates on the tongue, melding with brilliant-flavored rhubarb or black raspberries. The butterscotch pie, which she learned to cook from her grandmother, is more buttery than sweet, nothing at all like cloying pies made with pudding filling. And we won't even get into the hot apple dumpling . . .)

MAKES 4 SANDWICHES

2/3 cup all-purpose flour, plus more for dredging

4 1-inch-thick rounds of pork, cut from a pork tenderloin

2 cups buttermilk

2 large eggs

Vegetable oil for frying

2 cups crushed saltine crackers

4 large hamburger buns or hard rolls

Mustard and pickle chips, or other condiments of choice

Sprinkle a small amount of flour on a smooth, clean surface and use a meat pounder to pound each slice of pork until it is about ¼ inch thick.

Mix together the buttermilk, ⅔ cup flour, and eggs to make a paste. In a wide, shallow dish, cover the pounded slices of pork with this mixture. Cover and refrigerate for 12 to 16 hours.

Heat about 1 inch of oil to 350 degrees in a large cast-iron skillet.

Remove the soaked pork from the dish, letting any excess buttermilk paste drip away. Bread the pork with the crushed crackers, patting them so the crumbs adhere.

Ease each slice into the hot oil and fry until golden blond, turning them once. The total cooking time for each slice will be 6 to 8 minutes.

Sandwich each slice in a bun and dress with mustard and pickle chips or other condiments.

TENDERLOINS OF THE MIDWEST

In the heart of the heartland, between Nebraska's Midlands and the Wabash River Valley, a tenderloin is not just a cut of meat: it is a very important sandwich. When you ask for one in a café, drive-in, or diner, you can expect to get a slice of boneless pork loin that has been pounded flat, breaded, fried to a crisp, and planted in a bun (and, one hopes, dressed with mustard, pickle, lettuce, and tomato). The girth of the meat in a tenderloin ranges from generous, protruding maybe an inch past the circumference of the bun, to freakishly wide. In the latter category, you'll find tenderloins in which a plate-size pancake of pork extends so far beyond the bun that it is impossible to pick it up like a normal sandwich.

As is true of other emblematic regional passions, there are many substandard versions. The hapless hungry traveler is likely to find himself at a truck-stop counter facing a desiccated, Frisbee-flat tenderloin and wondering how such a sorry thing could inspire eaters' enthusiasm. The easy answer is to taste a good one.

While Iowa and Illinois and even Missouri have their share of excellent tenderloins, we believe the best are found in Indiana. That is most likely where they were invented, at Nick's Kitchen in Huntington (see page 112). Another magnificent Hoosier tenderloin is served in Brown County, south of Indianapolis, in the town of Gnaw Bone. Gnaw Bone Food & Fuel is a gas station, convenience store, bait shop, and great place to eat. Beyond the shelves of sundries is a large storage room now set up for indoor dining at picnic tables covered with green-checked oilcloth. The tables are surrounded by plastic bins of odd-lot bargain merchandise, including souvenir T-shirts from North Carolina and three-dollar audio CDs. Hot meals are served from 10:30 A.M. to 2 P.M., then again from 4 P.M. to 6 P.M.

The chef and owner, Beni Clevenger, credits the success of his outsize tenderloin to the fact that he cooks it in a Broaster. More commonly used to make chicken, a Broaster deep-fries food under pressure. "My tenderloin cooks from the inside out," Beni explains. "That keeps the pork plenty moist while the crust crisps up like the devil." He says he buys his meat just like anyone else around there — already cubed from the local IGA. "The less you mess with it, the better it will be," he says. "Don't be pounding the life out of it. Start with good meat and treat it gentle. That's the Gnaw Bone way to cook."

✳ Horseshoe Sandwich

Like beef on weck in Buffalo, New York (page 18), and beer-battered brain sandwiches in St. Louis (page 159), the horseshoe of Springfield, Illinois, is a local passion, little known and never encountered outside its home. Virtually every café, diner, and pub around the capital city serves this strange open-face sandwich, and in nearly as many forms as there are hoagies in New Jersey.

The original, as invented in 1928 at the Leland Hotel, was built around a slab of ham. Since then, hamburgers have become even more popular as the meat of choice. Other local options include corned beef, walleye, grilled vegetables, turkey, chicken, tomato, and loosemeats (see page 137). Downsized versions are known as ponyshoes, and at least one place in town offers breakfast horseshoes with eggs as the centerpiece.

Downstate foodies say that the sandwich got its name because it resembles an iron shoe being readied to get nailed onto a horse's hoof. The ham, set upon a couple of pieces of thick toast, is the shoe; French fries, arrayed around the ham, are the nails; and the platter on which the whole shebang is served is the blacksmith's anvil. What exactly the requisite cheese sauce represents in this explanation we cannot say.

D'Arcy's Pint is an Irish pub that makes the best horseshoes (not to mention shepherd's pie and Irish pot roast). There are twelve different versions of Springfield's sandwich on the menu, including a popular Buffalo chicken shoe served with blue cheese dressing and red hot sauce. If you are going to order—or make—a horseshoe for the first time, we recommend the classic ham.

Not all cheese sauces are made with beer, but we like it in our rendition of the dish because it gives the heavy-duty plate a yeasty bounce.

1½   cups shredded American cheese
1½   tablespoons butter
¼   teaspoon dry mustard
½   teaspoon Worcestershire sauce
2   large egg yolks
½   cup beer (lager)
4   slices Texas toast (bread cut double-thick and toasted)
2   thick slices cooked ham (3–4 ounces total)
2   cups French fries
     Paprika

Make the cheese sauce by melting the cheese and butter in a small saucepan over very low heat. Stir in the mustard and Worcestershire sauce. Beat together the egg yolks and beer in a small bowl and add this to the cheese. Stir constantly over medium-low heat as the mixture thickens. Just as it begins to bubble, remove it from the heat. You will have a little more than 1 cup.

Assemble each sandwich by placing 2 slices of Texas toast on a platter. Lay 1 ham slice over both pieces of toast. Strew 1 cup of the French fries over the ham. Dollop cheese sauce on the fries. Garnish with paprika to taste and serve.

✳✳ Hot Beef

LANGE'S CAFÉ ✳✳ **PIPESTONE, MINNESOTA**

Back in the 1960s, when the Langes were remodeling their café, they included a ceremonial moment in the construction process: the keys to the front door were dropped into wet cement. "Here's to never closing!" was the toast, and to make sure they remained true to the promise, lockless doors were installed. In the past four-plus decades, Lange's has remained open around the clock, every day. When you dine at this traveler's oasis in far southwestern Minnesota, you will find "trivia cards" that testify to the kitchen's commitment. One declares, "It takes 468,000 napkins, 58,600 jellies, 70,000 saltines, 990 pounds of peanut butter, 4,800 bottles of Heinz ketchup, and 40,000 coffee filters to serve you!" Another card lists 63,118 pounds of potatoes and 12,390 pounds of roast beef, which are the statistics that interest us the most, because Lange's hot beef sandwich is a heartland classic.

Understand that in the Upper Midwest, the term "hot beef" implies something a lot more wonderful than just some skinny flaps of roast beef under canned gravy on blah white bread. As locally treasured here as hickory-smoked pork is in North Carolina, hot beef is the meal you expect not only in every town café but also at a wedding banquet, a silver anniversary, and a church supper. The beef must be pot-roast tender, the mashed potatoes and gravy freshly made. So it is at Lange's Café, where the sandwich is built upon hearty slices of baked-that-morning bread.

When we asked Steve and Peg Lange to share their recipe, they told us not only how to assemble the sandwich but how to roast the beef and mix the gravy and mash the potatoes. We're going to leave out their instructions for mashed-potato making, having faith that you will not resort to a powdered-potato mix, and we'll also trust you either to bake your own or to buy really good, fresh bread for the base of the sandwich. But here is Lange's way of preparing beef and gravy.

MAKES 1 SANDWICH

6-8 thick slices Hot Beef (recipe follows)
2 thick slices fresh homemade white bread or good, freshly made artisanal bread
1 ice cream scoop of just-mashed potatoes
Hot Beef Gravy (recipe follows)

On a large plate, place the roast beef on 1 slice of bread, top with the other slice of bread, and cut the sandwich in half diagonally. Use an ice cream scoop to place a sphere of mashed potatoes between the two sandwich halves. Smother everything with gravy and serve.

Hot Beef

MAKES ENOUGH FOR 12 SANDWICHES

1 8- to 10-pound boneless beef brisket, cut in half

Preheat the oven to 200 degrees.

Place the brisket halves in a deep roasting pan. Add 3 inches of water and cover tightly with aluminum foil. Bake for 15 hours.

Remove the beef from the pan, reserving the cooking liquid. Let the roast sit for 1 hour. Trim away the fat.

Strain the liquid and refrigerate it until you are ready to make the gravy.

Hot Beef Gravy

MAKES ABOUT 4½ CUPS

Reserved cooking liquid from brisket
2 cups water
¼ cup beef base (available in specialty stores)
2 cups cold water
2 tablespoons all-purpose flour
2 tablespoons cornstarch
1 teaspoon Kitchen Bouquet (located in the spices section
  of the supermarket)

Remove the reserved cooking liquid from the refrigerator and carefully remove and discard the congealed fat from the top.

In a saucepan, combine 2 cups of the cooking liquid with 2 cups water and the beef base. Bring to a boil, stirring until it is lump-free. Add the 2 cups cold water, then stir in the flour and cornstarch. Return the mixture to a boil and stir in the Kitchen Bouquet.

Leftover gravy will keep, covered and refrigerated, for about a week and can be microwaved to reheat.

✳ Hot Brown

The sandwich known as a hot brown is served throughout Kentucky in different configurations. We've seen some with crabmeat and we've seen vegetarian versions without bacon, but the original formula is, in our opinion, just right: white turkey meat under a spill of sizzling cheese sauce, slices of tomato, and strips of bacon, all piled on toast. Utensils are required for this hot dish, which, strictly speaking, qualifies as a sandwich only because bread is part of the formula. The truly correct place to eat one is at the Brown Hotel, where it was invented in the 1920s. Here is the hotel's story of how it came to be.

In 1923, The Brown Hotel drew over 1200 guests each evening for its dinner dance. In the wee hours of the morning, the guests would grow tired of dancing and retire to the restaurant for a bite to eat. Guests were growing rapidly tired of the traditional ham and eggs, so Chef Fred Schmidt set out to create something new to tempt his guests' palates. Thus, the Hot Brown was born, an open-face turkey sandwich with bacon, pimento, and a delicate mornay sauce. Who could have guessed that this chef's dedication to service would start such an enduring and well-loved Louisville tradition . . . the Hot Brown.

MAKES 4 SANDWICHES

8	tablespoons (1 stick) butter
6	tablespoons all-purpose flour
3-3½	cups milk
6	tablespoons grated Parmesan cheese, plus more for topping
1	large egg, beaten
¼	cup whipped cream (optional)
	Salt and freshly ground pepper
8	slices white bread, toasted (may be trimmed)
16-20	slices roast turkey
8	slices beefsteak tomato
8	strips bacon, fried until crisp

Melt the butter in a heavy saucepan over medium heat and stir in the flour. Stir in milk and 3 cups of the Parmesan cheese and simmer the sauce until the mixture thickens. When it is smooth, add up to ½ cup more milk if the sauce is too thick.

Gradually stir in the beaten egg, making sure not to allow the sauce to boil. Remove the pan from the heat. Fold in the whipped cream if desired. Add salt and pepper to taste.

Preheat the broiler.

For each hot brown, place 2 slices of toast on a metal (or flameproof) dish or a baking pan. Cover the toast with a liberal amount of turkey. Pour a generous amount of cheese sauce over the turkey and toast. Sprinkle the sauce with additional Parmesan cheese. Place the dish or baking pan under the broiler for a few minutes, until the sauce is speckled brown and bubbly. Remove from the broiler. Top with 2 tomato slices and cross 2 pieces of bacon on top of the tomato. Serve immediately.

✳ Hot Pork Sandwich

There is no way to overestimate the importance of pork in Iowa. In his best-selling 1932 novel *State Fair,* author Phil Stong describes one of the central characters, a boar named Blue Boy, as "the finest hog that ever was," noting that "if Blue Boy proved to be the best Hampshire boar in Iowa, it followed that he would be the best Hampshire boar in the world . . . the finest hog in the universe."

One of our favorite things to do when we go to the Iowa State Fair in Des Moines is to visit the Swine Pavilion, where a sign notes that one out of every sixteen jobs in the state is pig-related. Iowa is the nation's top pork producer, and the fair abounds with ways to sample it on the stroll—as a barbecue or ham sandwich or sausage-on-a-stick—as well as sitting down inside the Pork Tent, operated by the Iowa Pork Producers. The tent's pièce de résistance is a pork chop. But not just any pork chop; it is an *Iowa* pork chop, well over an inch thick and weighing approximately 1 pound. If skinny super-market flaps of meat are your idea of a pork chop, this glistening Gargantua, hot off the grill, is a revelation. It is sweet and juicy, fine-grained and dense, but supple enough to slice with the flimsy plastic knife provided, and satisfying beyond measure. The men who cook the chops on grills outside the tent wear aprons that boast of "the other white meat," but no other meat we know, white or red, has such fathomless succulence.

Any time of year other than during the state fair, you can sit down and enjoy just such a magnificent hunk of pork at the Iowa Machine Shed on the outskirts of Urbandale. In fact, there are eight Machine Shed restaurants in the heartland, the Urbandale branch adjoining Living History Farms, a celebration of rural life in the form of restored log cabins, Native American crafts displays, and a whole small town built to look as it would have looked in 1875. The Machine Shed is a culinary ode to the old-fashioned American farmer. Its interior is crowded with turn-of-the-century farm implements, seed bags, and vintage advertisements for country-style products. The staff dresses in farmhand attire (but clean!). Foremost among the meats is pork.

The chop is superb, and you can get a great butterflied pork chop sandwich, but we also love a big old hot pork sandwich, the recipe for which is simplicity itself. The Machine

Shed's recipe says that the pork can be seasoned with "any additional seasonings you prefer." We like rosemary and thyme, but there is nothing wrong with a bath of your favorite barbecue sauce. The sandwich is served on a choice of white, wheat, or marbled rye. Side it with mashed potatoes.

MAKES 4 TO 6 SANDWICHES

1	tablespoon olive oil or vegetable oil
1	2-pound boneless pork roast (loin or center cut)
1	tablespoon pork or chicken base (available in specialty stores) or chicken bouillon
2	tablespoons cornstarch, plus more if needed
	Seasonings to taste (see headnote)
8-12	slices white, whole wheat, or marbled rye bread

Heat a large skillet over medium-high heat and add the oil. Add the pork roast and brown each side, then remove it from the skillet and place it in a Crock-Pot or other slow cooker. (Reserve the oil in the skillet.) Cover the pork with water and add the pork or chicken base or bouillon and the seasonings. Cook on low until tender, about 6 hours, or until it reaches an internal temperature of 180 degrees (the optimal temperature so the meat is fall-apart tender).

To make pan gravy, take ⅓ cup of the water from the Crock-Pot and use it to deglaze the pan that you browned the roast in. Mix the cornstarch and ¼ cup water together in a small bowl. Bring the deglazed liquid to a boil over medium-high heat and stir in the cornstarch mixture. Cook, stirring, until the gravy is thickened. When ready to serve, pull the pork roast apart with forks or your fingers and place the meat between slices of your choice of bread. Smother the sandwich with gravy and serve.

Hot Roast Beef

Tipster Charles Cramer wrote us a note a while ago, insisting that we visit Shiek's Sandwich Shop in Torrington, Connecticut. He wasn't the first correspondent to sing its praises, but the former Torringtonian, now living in the orbit of Boston, made us an offer we couldn't refuse: "If you try it out and feel as though I've led you astray, I will gladly and willingly reimburse you for your meals."

Shiek's signature hot roast beef isn't just roast beef that is hot. It is roast beef in a sandwich that also has a distinct hot-pepper flavor. It's not ferociously incendiary by any means: the peppers included are the relatively tame bull's horns, those pale green, elongated pods found in supermarkets everywhere, which are most often fried to go with sausage or used in stir-fry dishes. (They are also known as banana peppers or Italian frying peppers.) At Shiek's they are oven-roasted until they are tender and smoky-flavored, an ideal companion for rare roast beef. The combination of peppers and beef (and provolone and grilled onions and mayonnaise and mustard) is so compelling that Mr. Cramer declared he thinks nothing of driving from Boston to Torrington for this sandwich, even though he has access to the very excellent Kelly's and other good roast beef sandwiches in his Beantown backyard.

Hot roast beef is just one of the many dishes that have made Shiek's a destination for diner lovers over the past thirty-five years. Also known for its terrific chili dogs, Shiek's looks like a corner hash house but treats ingredients like the Cordon Bleu. Chef and proprietor Gary Arnold told us that he hand-trims, ties, and cooks his beef rounds, hand-slicing 175 pounds per week. His advice for making the sandwich is to start with very rare roast beef so that it can be heated on the grill and still come off pink. His other admonition is to use top-quality bread. He gets fresh-baked rolls cooked in a steam oven that leaves them crusty on the outside and soft enough inside to absorb the juices of the roast beef.

MAKES 1 SANDWICH

6 thin slices rare roast beef
2 slices provolone cheese
1 hard roll, sliced and ready to load
¼ cup sliced Italian frying (banana) peppers, roasted (see page 89), peeled, seeded, and stemmed (1 pepper)
Suggested additions: grilled onions, lettuce, mayonnaise, mustard

Place the roast beef in a hot, lightly oiled skillet and cook it just long enough to warm it, no longer than 2 minutes.

Place the cheese on the bottom of the roll and pile the hot roast beef atop it. Place the peppers on top of the meat and top with whatever additions you like. Place the other half of the roll on top and serve hot.

✳ Italian Beef

HARRY CARAY'S ✳ CHICAGO, ILLINOIS

In Chicago the Italian beef sandwich is as much a part of culinary culture as deep-dish pan pizza and Marshall Field's Frango Mint Chocolates. It is called Italian because the first people to serve it were of Italian descent, but its popularity is citywide among a culturally diverse population. Thin-sliced beef sopped in gravy and stuffed into the absorbent maw of a fresh loaf of good French or Italian bread is the premier street food in the toddlin' town, and while many stand-up purveyors sell very good versions of it, there is something extra-special about having your beef at Harry Caray's.

Known primarily for its stupendous steaks, this lusty restaurant was named for the man who was the voice of the Chicago Cubs (and the restaurant's founder). Here Italian beef sandwiches are served in high style in the barroom. While more formal meals are accompanied by fine wines and arrayed on thick white tablecloths in ad-joining dining rooms, the bar is the place people come for lunch, for after-work li-bations, for an informal dinner, and for intense baseball watching while they dine. The bar itself is exactly 60 feet 6 inches long—the Major League's official distance from the pitcher's rubber to home plate. Here are twelve televisions, including a 120-inch big screen on which "Sing Along with Harry" is featured at 7:30 every night: a tribute to the founder's unfailing rendition of "Take Me Out to the Ball Game" during the seventh-inning stretch of each home game he announced.

It is in the bar from 11:30 A.M. to 4 P.M. every day that a sandwich cart is rolled out and sandwiches are made to order. You can get prime rib or turkey, but it's the roast beef we like best. Harry's dresses the beef the traditional way but offers a different twist on the formula in the form of smoked mozzarella.

MAKES 4 SANDWICHES

       2   cups water
       1   beef bouillon cube
       2   celery stalks, sliced
       1   carrot, sliced
       1   Spanish onion, chopped
       1   teaspoon dried oregano
     ½   teaspoon dried basil
     ½   teaspoon freshly ground pepper
          Salt
     ¼   cup olive oil
     ½   green bell pepper, seeded and sliced lengthwise into 4 pieces
     ½   yellow bell pepper, seeded and sliced lengthwise into 4 pieces
     ½   red bell pepper, seeded and sliced lengthwise into 4 pieces
       1   long loaf French or Italian bread, cut into 4 pieces
       2   pounds thinly sliced roast beef
       8   1½-ounce slices smoked mozzarella cheese

To make the jus, combine the water, bouillon cube, celery, carrot, onion, oregano, basil, pepper, and salt to taste in a medium saucepan. Simmer the mixture over medium heat for 20 minutes. Strain the jus and return it to the saucepan. Keep warm.

Preheat the oven to 350 degrees.

In a large skillet, heat the oil over medium heat and sauté the peppers until they are soft.

Slice the pieces of bread in half lengthwise, leaving each piece hinged. Stir the sliced roast beef in the jus for 30 seconds. Fill each piece of bread with soaked roast beef. Top the meat with 1 slice each of the green, yellow, and red bell peppers. Cover each sandwich with 2 slices of the smoked mozzarella. Place the sandwiches on a baking sheet and bake for 5 minutes, or until the cheese is melted. Serve with the jus for dipping.

✳ Italian Roast Pork

TONY LUKE'S ✳ PHILADELPHIA, PENNSYLVANIA

Philadelphia is best known for its cheesesteak, but there is another sandwich of brotherly love that cannot be ignored: Italian roast pork. Roast pork is dished out by some of the same places that serve first-rate steaks, where it is a similarly sloppy, gravy-dripping torpedo of meat and cheese, but Tony Luke's and a few other joints around the city include one sensational addition: broccoli rabe sautéed with plenty of garlic in olive oil. The result is a sandwich with a beautiful balance of flavors, even if it is a royal mess to eat.

Tony Luke's is barely a restaurant. Typical of local sandwich shops, service is do-it-yourself style. Place your order at the counter, pay, wait to be called, and go get it. Seating is minimal in a semi-al-fresco area near the counter, where the walls are profusely decorated in classic Delaware Valley hoagie-shop style, meaning a gallery of autographed 8-x-10-inch publicity photos of celebrities from entertainment, sports (especially boxing), and politics.

There are no plates. Sandwiches are delivered into your hands wrapped in paper in brown bags. At table, on picnic bench or lap, the bag and wrapping paper become accidental targets for all the sliced pork and broccoli rabe that tumble out as the prodigious sandwich is hoisted to eat.

MAKES 2 VERY LARGE SANDWICHES; SERVES 2 TO 4

2 12-inch lengths fresh, chewy Italian bread with a sturdy crust (not flaky)
4 slices provolone cheese
   Sautéed Broccoli Rabe (recipe follows)
1 pound thinly sliced pork shoulder, cooked according to the directions on page 190, with juices to keep the slices moist
2 teaspoons dried oregano
   Optional condiments: jarred giardiniera, jarred hot peppers, roasted red bell peppers (see page 89)

Slice the loaves of bread lengthwise. Lay half of the provolone on the bottom of each loaf. Immediately add a layer of warm broccoli rabe, which will help soften the cheese. Top with a sheaf of warm roast pork. Season with the oregano and add condiments if desired.

Sautéed Broccoli Rabe

MAKES ENOUGH FOR 2 SANDWICHES

- 1 bunch (about 1 pound) broccoli rabe, stems trimmed
- 2 tablespoons olive oil
- 2-3 garlic cloves, slightly mashed
- 1 cup chicken stock

Thoroughly wash the broccoli rabe, then cut it into pieces no longer than 3 inches.

In a large skillet, heat the oil over medium-high heat and sauté the garlic until it begins to soften. Add the chicken stock and bring to a simmer. Add the broccoli rabe, cover, reduce the heat to low, and cook for 45 minutes, or until tender, stirring occasionally and adding a little more chicken stock or water if necessary to make sure the broccoli rabe stays moist. Remove it from the pan and drain off the excess liquid. Remove the garlic cloves if desired. Keep warm.

HOW TO EAT A REALLY MESSY SANDWICH

Some sandwiches are so sloppy that they require a special ingestion technique. We are not referring to those that demand a knife and fork and a well-anchored position in a chair at a table. We are talking about sandwiches that are eaten by hand but are so messy that they run the risk of disintegrating all over your lap (if you're sitting) or your shoes (if you are standing up). We learned precisely how to eat one from Chris Pacelli, Jr., who owns Al's #1 Italian Beef in Chicago, Illinois, with his brothers Chuck and Terry.

It is important to understand that Al's is a restaurant with no tables and chairs. Like so many of Chicago's street-food purveyors, it has an order counter where you pick up your food and a waist-high ledge around the edge of the place to which you take the food to eat. Some such places have stools for sitting at the ledge, but standing is the traditional way.

"Assume the stance," Chris honks in pure Chicago style, positioning himself at an Al's ledge. "Put your feet apart and slide 'em back like you are going to be frisked. Put your two elbows on the counter and put both your hands on the sandwich, thumbs underneath." When he stands in this position with his mitts enveloping a Big Al's beef sandwich — a shaft of fresh-baked bread loaded with warm sliced meat, garnished with sweet roasted peppers and hot giardiniera relish, and soaked with natural gravy — he looks like a giddy strangler with his fingers wrapped around a neck. "Now, bring it to your face." He pauses for a delicious moment when the sandwich is close enough to smell its warm, beefy bouquet. His elbows never leave the counter as he opens wide to yank off a juicy chaw, then pulls what's left away to a nice viewing distance, relishing the sight of it and the savor in his mouth. "See how all the juice drips on the counter, not on your shoes or shirt? That's because of the stance!"

Liver 'n' Onion Sandwich with Firecracker Sauce

OLD POST OFFICE ✳ **EDISTO ISLAND, SOUTH CAROLINA**

Ask any food-savvy person in the Charleston area where to eat meals that sing of South Carolina's coastal culture, and chances are good you will be directed to the Old Post Office on Edisto Island. Located in a building that in fact used to be the island's post office, the restaurant has garnered national fame for its imaginative and delicious variations of Lowcountry cooking, and chef Philip Bardin has been recognized as one of American cuisine's creative pillars.

Chef Bardin changes his menu to reflect the spectacular vegetable crops of Edisto as well as the seafood caught around here, but certain favorites of his transcend area taste. For example, his roast duck is one of the best you will eat anywhere; his "fussed-over pork chop" and "ultimate filet mignon" are unsurpassed. And when we asked him to supply us with a sandwich recipe that was one of his very favorites, he stunned us with this dazzling variation on good old liver 'n' onions.

Like ourselves, Philip is a liver lover, but we must say that what elevates the traditional combo into the pantheon is the Firecracker Sauce. This sauce is also used by the Old Post Office kitchen to top the local flounder, and it goes without saying that the better the salsa used, the tastier the sauce. In any case, you want it hot!

1   cup buttermilk
     Salt
2-4 ounces beef liver, sliced ½ inch thick
1   cup all-purpose flour
1   tablespoon Italian seasoning
     Freshly ground pepper
1   tablespoon butter
1   tablespoon olive oil
1   tablespoon fresh lemon juice
1   onion, sliced into medium-thick rings
4   slices pumpernickel bread, toasted
½   cup Firecracker Sauce (recipe follows)
4   thick slices provolone cheese

Combine the buttermilk and 1 tablespoon salt in a wide, shallow bowl and soak the beef liver in it for 1 hour. Drain the liver.

Combine the flour, Italian seasoning, and 1 teaspoon pepper in another wide, shallow bowl. Dredge the liver in the flour mixture. Heat the butter and olive oil in a skillet and pan-fry the liver until it is cooked through, about 3 minutes per side. Remove the liver and season with salt, pepper, and lemon juice.

Preheat the broiler.

Heat the skillet over medium-high heat, adding more olive oil and butter if necessary, then add the onion rings and cook until soft, about 4 minutes.

Place 2 slices of the toasted pumpernickel bread on a baking sheet. Divide the liver between the bread. Top the liver with the onions and a thick topping of the firecracker sauce. Top each sandwich with 2 slices provolone and melt it under the broiler. Top with the other slice of toast, cut in half, and serve.

Firecracker Sauce

The sauce tastes best if made a day ahead, refrigerated, and then reheated.

MAKES 1 CUP

1   tablespoon olive oil
2   Roma tomatoes, thinly sliced
½   onion, thinly sliced
1   jalapeño pepper, thinly sliced
    Pinch of sugar (optional)
1   tablespoon Frank's RedHot Original Cayenne Pepper Sauce
    or Tabasco sauce
½   cup fresh salsa or tomato puree

Heat the oil in a medium skillet. Sauté the tomatoes, onion, and jalapeño until they are tender. You may want to add a touch of sugar if the tomatoes are underripe. Add the hot sauce and salsa or puree and simmer over low heat for about 5 minutes.

Lobster Roll, Hot or Cold

MAINE DINER ✳ WELLS, MAINE

Although the hot lobster roll was invented in Connecticut (see page 136) and remains a southern New England specialty, one of the best versions we've found is Down East at the Maine Diner. While we are the first to admit that it is all too easy to be sidetracked by the diner's ambrosial baked lobster pie as well as its outstanding "clamorama" dinner, those in search of lobster roll excellence need look no further.

While the typical hot lobster roll comes with the meat already gilded with melted butter, the Maine Diner's version is even simpler than that: plain, warm lobster piled into a toasted bun, presented with a cup of drawn butter on the side. "Somebody from Rhode Island suggested the buttered roll many years ago," proprietor Dick Henry told us. "But we found that if we served the meat already buttered, the bun fell apart." So when you are presented with this beauteous delight, you can either pour all the butter all over the sandwich, risking bun disintegration, or you can simply pick chunks of meat and shreds of toasted bread from the plate and dip them in the cup of butter as you wish. Either way, he advises, "Have a knife and fork handy. And plenty of napkins or a small towel."

While not essential, split-top hot dog rolls with a flat surface on each side are by far the best kind of bun to use. They are made for grilling . . . in butter, of course!

Hot Lobster Roll

About 1 cup hot melted butter
2   split-top hot dog rolls
1½ cups warm lobster meat, in bite-size pieces

Butter a skillet or griddle with some of the melted butter and grill the rolls on both sides until the outside is crisp and light brown. Fill the rolls with lobster meat and serve them with a cup of melted butter on the side.

Cold Lobster Salad Roll

More typical of Maine cafés, and beautifully made at the Maine Diner, is the lobster salad roll, aka cold lobster roll. When you make this at home, you can add a layer of lettuce and doll up the lobster salad with bits of celery or pickle; you can even flavor the mayonnaise and make it aïoli.

Serve with pickles and potato chips.

MAKES 2 ROLLS

¾   cup lobster meat, cooled, in bite-size pieces
    Mayonnaise
    Butter
2   split-top hot dog rolls

Mix the lobster meat with mayonnaise to taste. Butter a skillet or griddle and grill the rolls on both sides until the outside is golden brown. Fill the warm rolls with the lobster salad and serve.

LOBSTER ROLLS

A lobster roll makes lobster eating easy. No cracking of the shell, no sucking, poking, or picking to get at the meat. Just hoist the bun and enjoy: lobster-lover's heaven!

Lobster rolls are uncomplicated sandwiches, basically lobster meat surrounded by bread. The quality of the lobster is of paramount concern: you want it freshly cooked and just extracted from the shell, and you want a good mix of tail meat, which is juicy and resilient, and claw meat, which is tender. Most lobster rolls are made in a New England–style hot dog bun that splits apart at the top and has flat sides that can be toasted in a film of butter on a short-order grill. Some are served wrapped in wax paper, others in little cardboard boats that tend to squeeze the sides together, like the action of a push-up brassiere, causing the bun to bulge and forcing the meat upward, making it appear more abundantly endowed than it really is. Sometimes the meat is on a bed of lettuce, which can seem like padding but also can serve the admirable purpose of keeping the moist lobster meat from sogging the bun.

The big issue among lobster roll connoisseurs is, hot or cold? The cold lobster roll is the time-honored Maine-coast way of doing it: lobster meat bound with mayonnaise and bits of celery loaded into a bun that may or may not be toasted. But in 1929 Harry Perry, of Milford, Connecticut, came up with something different. To please a lobster-loving customer at his seafood shack on the Post Road, Perry created the hot lobster roll: nothing but warm picked meat bathed in butter and cosseted in a bun. It was such a success that Perry's shack soon sported a sign boasting that it was HOME OF THE FAMOUS LOBSTER ROLL, and his ridiculously rich creation became what *Connecticut Magazine* editor Charles Monagan has called "Connecticut's greatest contribution to the world of regional cuisine."

Warm lobster rolls tend to be impossible to eat, start to finish, without major sandwich disintegration. That is because the best of them contain meat that is sopping with warm melted butter that makes your chin and hands glisten, and by the time you are halfway through, the bun itself has become so buttery that it starts to fall apart. This is a problem only if you haven't planned ahead and taken your bites over a paper plate or other good catchall surface from which you can pick buttery, lobstery pieces of bread to conclude the meal. Today you still find more hot lobster rolls in Connecticut than Down East along the coast, but the warm luxury of Mr. Perry's creation has made its way to menus all along Yankee shores.

✳✳ Loosemeats

A loosemeats is a sloppy Joe without slop. Ground beef is cooked loose—unpattied—seasoned, drained, and bunned, with no sauce. Cheese may be included, along with pickle and mustard —a sort of remix of the cheeseburger with fragmented harmony. Unike grits, of which there is never one, it is a food spoken of with singular/plural ambivalence. Usually one sandwich is a loosemeats; a batch in the kitchen or a bowlful without the bun is loosemeats.

It can be slightly tricky to find loosemeats in northwest Iowa, even though it is more popular than hamburgers, because it has so many aliases. At Bob's Drive-Inn of Le Mars, it is called a Tavern. Other names include Big T, Charlie Boy, and Tastee. Sticklers for historical veracity prefer the term "Tavern," because that is what it was called when David Heglin first served it in 1924 at a twenty-five-seat Sioux City restaurant he ran called Ye Old Tavern. (Two years later the first Maid-Rite eatery opened in Muscatine, at the eastern end of the state, serving the nearly identical sandwich, called a Maid-Rite.) In 1934 Abe Kaled bought Ye Old Tavern, changed its name to Ye Olde Tavern, and also tinkered with the formula for ground beef on a bun. Kaled and his wife, Bertha, sold Taverns for a dime apiece. (Loosemeats now sell for $1.30 to $1.50 in most restaurants.) Their restaurant inspired imitations for miles around, and by the time Ye Olde Tavern closed in 1971, Sioux Cityans were smitten with the sandwich.

Like barbecue in the ranchland east of Santa Barbara or Brunswick stew in southern Virginia, loosemeats is a favorite thing to serve at fund-raising suppers. It continues to be a staple on school lunch menus, and it is served by virtually every drive-in restaurant and bar throughout the counties of Sioux, Plymouth, Cherokee, and Woodbury.

A loosemeats is especially well suited for bar food because it is always presented as it was at Ye Olde Tavern: wrapped in wax paper, never on a plate. At Sioux City's Miles Inn, where the sandwich is called a Charlie Boy (after Charlie Miles, son of founder John Miles, the bricklayer who built the inn in 1925), it is the only food you can buy other than Beer Nuts and potato chips. Sitting at the bar, you have a view of the steam box in which the meat is kept and of Charlie Boys being assembled as you drink beer from a frosted goblet. Miles Inn's Charlie Boys are small and addictive, their fine-grind meat so soft and gently seasoned that it hits the tongue as smooth as cream.

Tastee Inn & Out, just around the corner from Miles Inn, calls its loosemeats sandwich a Tastee and also sells Tastee meat to go at $3.99 per pound. Tastee is a classic American drive-in in every way except for the fact that, like Bob's, it doesn't serve hamburgers. Opened by the Calligan family in 1955, Tastee has become nearly as famous for its onion chips as for seasoned beef. The chips are like onion rings but made from large sections of a petaled onion that retain sweet vegetable crunch inside their crust. As for the Tastee, it has a zing we want to call tomato-like, except for the fact that every loosemeats cook unconditionally abjures tomatoes.

It came as no surprise as we explored loosemeats culture that virtually every restaurant's recipe is a closely held secret. Like Cincinnati chili, each version is a little different, but the basic principles are the same. While restaurant chefs steam their meat, we have gotten fine results at home using our oldest, best-seasoned cast-iron skillet and this recipe. Loosemeats makes a swell casual-party dish because it can be held in a slow cooker and people can make their own sandwiches just the way they like them.

2   tablespoons vegetable oil
1   pound ground chuck
    Salt
$^2/_3$ cup finely chopped onion
1   tablespoon red wine vinegar
    Freshly ground pepper
4   hamburger buns, warmed for a few seconds in the microwave
4   slices American cheese
    Pickle chips
    Prepared yellow mustard (optional)

Heat the oil in a large, heavy cast-iron skillet over medium heat. Add the ground beef and use a spatula and/or a wooden spoon to press and worry it into very small bits. As you are worrying the meat, add 1 tablespoon salt and the onion. When the meat is light brown, drain off any excess fat; then stir in the vinegar and pepper. Add enough water to nearly cover the meat. Simmer, uncovered, stirring occasionally, for 15 to 20 minutes. The water should be boiled off, but if it isn't, use a slotted spoon to transfer the meat from the pan to a bowl. The meat should be slightly moist but not drippy.

Scoop one fourth of the warm beef mixture onto the bottom of each warmed bun. Add the cheese, which will semimelt from the meat's heat. Place pickle chips atop the cheese and apply mustard to the top of the bun, if desired. Place the tops over the cheese and serve immediately.

Meaty Chili and Cheddar

CLEMENTINE ✳ LOS ANGELES, CALIFORNIA

Raise your hand if you know that April is National Grilled Cheese Month. So it was decreed by some cheese council or other, but we were ignorant of the holiday until chef Annie Milar of Clementine so informed us. Clementine is a neighborhood bakery-café in the Westwood–Century City part of Los Angeles that for several years now has been marking the occasion with an annual monthlong festival that features a different grilled cheese sandwich on the menu every day.

Annie explained that each celebration so far has been unique. Because April also happens to be National Poetry Month, one year's festivities included a grilled cheese haiku competition. Another year inspired the creation of an animated flip book of grilled cheese sandwiches. In 2005 the theme was Destination: Grilled Cheese, for which Clementine offered customers a grilled cheese passport listing sandwiches from many lands. Looking just like an official government passport, this document included space to be stamped every time a customer ordered the featured sandwich and space for a photograph of the customer, provided by the restaurant's Polaroid camera.

Of all the grilled cheese sandwiches Clementine's kitchen makes, Chef Annie's favorite is meaty chili and cheddar, variations of which sometimes include a hot dog and go by the name of Coney Island Grilled Cheese. She describes the sandwich as "gooey, sloppy, and delicious." As Annie notes, you can make fewer sandwiches and freeze any leftover chili for future use.

MAKES 6 SANDWICHES

Butter for spreading
12 large slices country white bread
1 pound white cheddar cheese (medium-sharp), thinly sliced
Meaty Chili (recipe follows)

Butter 1 side of each slice of bread and place them butter side down. Divide the cheese evenly among the bread slices. Top each of 6 slices with about ⅓ cup chili. Top with the other 6 slices bread, cheese side down. The sandwiches can be assembled a day ahead, wrapped tightly in plastic, and refrigerated.

TO COOK THE SANDWICHES: Place a batch of sandwiches in a large skillet and heat slowly. When the sandwiches are brown and crispy on one side, flip them over and cook until brown and crispy on the other side, about 10 minutes per side. Repeat with the remaining sandwiches. Cut in half and serve hot.

✳✳ Meaty Chili

For the best flavor, make the chili at least 1 day and up to 3 days ahead.

MAKES 2½ CUPS

1	pound coarsely ground beef
1-2	tablespoons vegetable oil, if needed
1	small onion, finely chopped
1	garlic clove, minced
1½	tablespoons salt
1½	tablespoons ancho chile powder
1½	tablespoons chile powder (preferably from New Mexico)
1½	teaspoons dried oregano
1	teaspoon ground cumin
1½	tablespoons finely chopped pickled jalapeños, or to taste
1½	tablespoons unsweetened cocoa powder
1½	tablespoons dark brown sugar
1½	tablespoons cornmeal
½	cup water
1	cup canned crushed tomatoes

Brown the meat in a medium pan over medium-high heat, using the oil if the meat is lean. Pour off the excess fat. Add the onion and sauté until softened, about 3 minutes, then add the garlic. Stir in the salt, chile powders, oregano, cumin, jalapeños, cocoa powder, and brown sugar. Add the cornmeal, water, and tomatoes. Reduce the heat to low and simmer for 20 minutes, stirring occasionally.

Mighty Ity

SUPER DUPER WEENIE ✳ FAIRFIELD, CONNECTICUT

Trained at the Culinary Institute of America and employed as chef in one of Connecticut's most esteemed high-ticket Italian restaurants, Gary Zemola craved running a diner. Unable to afford a classic streamliner, he found a decrepit food-service truck and reinvented it as Super Duper Weenie. Now a permanent building just off I-95, Gary's dream come true has become America's foremost tutorial in wienerology, featuring consummate variations on the theme: a Chicagoan (lettuce, tomato, mustard, celery salt, relish, pickle), a Dixie (chili and sweet slaw), a Californian (chili, onions, cheese, relish), a New Yorker (sauerkraut, onion sauce, mustard, relish), and the signature dish, a New Englander, which is topped with the neighborhood's traditional condiment constellation of sauerkraut, bacon, mustard, sweet relish, and raw onion. When you perch on a stool to eat one of these magnificent hot dogs, Gary will probably regale you with stories of a recent trip he has taken to explore steamed cheeseburgers north of New Haven, pig sandwiches in Memphis, or Italian beef in Chicago.

As the name of the restaurant suggests, weenies are the primary attraction. But Gary is a prodigious chef, and nothing on the menu is ordinary. Soups are grandma-good, French fries are some of the best anywhere, and the sandwich menu includes one of the great cheesesteaks outside of Philadelphia as well as the superb Mighty Ity sausage sandwich. When Gary gave us the recipe for this one, he said that he felt the key to making it great—beyond using excellent ingredients—is time. "Don't rush anything when making a Mighty Ity," he said. "Let the flavors meld."

1 pork sausage patty or 2 links pork sausage
1 teaspoon extra-virgin olive oil, if needed
1 green or red bell pepper, seeded and cut into ¼-inch-wide lengthwise strips
1 medium Spanish onion, cut into ¼-inch-wide lengthwise strips
1-2 garlic cloves, smashed
1-2 slices provolone cheese or mozzarella cheese
1 Portuguese roll or hard roll of choice, sliced in half horizontally
Salt and freshly ground pepper

Heat a heavy cast-iron skillet over medium heat. Add the sausage, allowing the fat to render. Cook for 3 to 4 minutes, flip, and cook the other side for another 3 to 4 minutes. Remove the sausage from the pan and set aside.

If the sausage was too lean to leave a good film of oil in the pan, add the olive oil. Add the bell pepper, onion, and garlic. Reduce the heat to low and cook, without stirring, until the vegetables are softened. Stir once, just enough to scrape the bits of pork and fat from the bottom of the pan, and turn the vegetables over. Cook until the onion is translucent, the pepper is soft and browned, and the garlic is slightly golden.

Add the sausage to the pan and place the cheese on top of it. When the cheese is melted and the sausage heated through, assemble the sandwich by placing the sausage on the bottom of the roll and topping it with the hot vegetables from the pan. Season with salt and pepper to taste, place the top of the roll on the vegetables, and serve.

✳ Milano

SAND-WEDGE ✳ GEORGETOWN, CONNECTICUT

The name Sand-Wedge has multiple meanings. Southern Fairfield County in Connecticut and Westchester County in New York know the hero sandwich (grinder, submarine, po' boy) as a "wedge," and wedges are a specialty of this deli kitchen. The other meaning of the term is apparent the moment you walk in. The walls are covered with pictures and souvenirs that are odes to former proprietor Shannon Campbell's favorite sport, golf. Hanging from the ceiling are over 250 golf towels from courses around the world, brought back to George-town by customers who share Shannon's passion. When he was pondering a name for his new restaurant just before opening it in 1998 and his brother came up with "Sand-Wedge," Shannon was ecstatic. It was the perfect title to describe the two things he wanted to celebrate in this little place by the side of Route 7: golf and sandwiches.

Sand-Wedge is mostly a take-out restaurant, with just four little tables inside where people can sit, unwrap their lunch, and eat. A huge menu hangs behind the counter, and once you've chosen the sandwich you want, it's astonishing just how fast the people working here can assemble it, even if it's one of the specialty combos of multiple ingredients.

The cold-cut creations are just fine, but some of the hot sandwiches are extra-spe-cial. One such beauty is Shannon's personal favorite, the Milano, rich with fried eggplant, spinach, mozzarella, and ricotta cheese tightly enclosed inside the wrap of your choice. (Our choice is the tomato wrap.)

1 medium eggplant

2 large eggs

1 teaspoon salt

½ teaspoon freshly ground pepper

Italian-seasoned dried bread crumbs

1 cup freshly washed spinach, coarsely chopped

Vegetable oil for frying

¼ cup shredded mozzarella cheese

¼ cup ricotta cheese

1 large sandwich wrap of choice (see headnote)

Peel the eggplant and cut it into slices about ½ inch thick. Beat the eggs in a wide, shallow bowl and stir the salt and pepper into them. Dip the slices of eggplant into the egg mixture and dredge them in the bread crumbs, making sure each slice is fully covered.

In a small bowl in a microwave, or in a small saucepan on the stovetop, steam the still-wet spinach until it is limp.

Heat about ½ inch of oil to 360 degrees in a large, deep skillet. Fry the eggplant until golden brown, turning the slices once, 2 to 3 minutes total. Remove with a slotted spoon and drain on paper towels.

Preheat the broiler.

Spread the mozzarella cheese and ricotta cheese over the wrap and set the wrap under the broiler just until the mozzarella melts; watch carefully so it doesn't burn. Remove the wrap and heap on the eggplant and spinach. Wrap tightly, but not so tightly that the cheese oozes out.

Cut in half and serve.

✱✱ Milk Toast

DRAKE'S SANDWICH SHOP ✱✱ ANN ARBOR, MICHIGAN

Alas, Drake's is no more. For decades this sandwich shop in the heart of Ann Arbor, Michigan, supplied students and townies not only with excellent lunch-counter sandwiches but also with beautiful layer cakes, candies, and morning pecan rolls, as well as a full soda-fountain repertoire of ice cream treats. When we first encountered it in the middle of the twentieth century, it already seemed like a relic, and although it was a place that time forgot, we were shocked when it closed its doors in 1993. It had become such a beloved institution that there is today a lovely Drake's tribute site on the Internet (www.joedurrance.com /drakes_tribute/index.html), which includes the sounds of Drake's before it closed, customers' memories, pictures, and an interview with proprietor Truman Tibbals, who had been there since the 1920s.

Drake's sandwich menu included many items as primordial as the place itself: cucumber sandwiches, jelly and cream cheese, and the plainest (and most perfect) grilled cheese on white ever slid off a grill. Also listed among the sandwiches was an item that has virtually disappeared from menus everywhere: milk toast. Once available in most fine hotels and made by mothers for sickly children, milk toast is nursery comfort food par excellence. For a cold winter's day or for a midnight snack after a long, hard night, few dishes provide the kind of succor this one does.

Nor is anything easier to prepare. The ingredients, after all, are milk and toast. But some subtleties and variations are worth considering.

The first rule of making good milk toast is to toast the bread properly. It ought to be white bread, nothing fancy, but preferably homemade and sliced thick. Toast it only until it is light brown and the exterior is crisp but the inside is still tender.

The toast should be torn, not cut, into bite-size pieces before it is put into the bowl. This is important, as it eliminates the need for sawing and cutting while eating. It is vital to the spirit of the dish that the consumption of milk toast be baby-food easy.

The milk (or cream, if you want it super-luxurious) must not be boiled. Heat it so it is hot enough to melt the butter but not scald the tongue.

Finally, although simplicity is the essence of the dish, there are some nice little variations: sprinkle the milk toast with a tablespoon or two of cinnamon sugar or maple sugar, or drizzle on a thin layer of honey.

SERVES 1

2 slices thick white bread, lightly toasted
1 cup milk, cream, or half-and-half
2 tablespoons butter
Salt

Tear the toast into bite-size pieces and place them in a wide, shallow bowl. Warm the milk. Pour it over the toast and immediately dot with the butter. Sprinkle with salt to taste. Serve immediately.

Milwaukee Reuben

MCBOB'S ✳ MILWAUKEE, WISCONSIN

Most people think of Milwaukee as the city of great fish fries, which it is, and of America's best custard, which it is also, and of butter burgers, which are pretty fine too. Not to mention beer. But Milwaukee has another claim to fame, little known to outsiders and yet deeply appreciated by the local culinary cognoscenti. That is corned beef. Here you will find some of the most delicious corned beef, and hot corned beef sandwiches, anywhere in the U.S.A.

In fact, we went to McBob's for its fish fry, which is something to rave about—a choice of perch, walleye, or grouper, or a combination of two or three, the crisp-fried fish served over a layer of thin, oniony potato pancakes. The two Milwaukeeans who clued us in to McBob's, Jessica Zierten and Brad Warsh, insisted we try the corned beef too. Wow, are we glad we did! And we are especially glad that Bob Rubner shared his recipe with us. He even explained how McBob's prepares its corned beef.

"We start by making sure we use the best-quality corned beef available," Bob said. He slow-cooks the beef at 250 degrees for at least 12 hours—until it's fall-apart tender—then holds it at 140 degrees until it's time to start making the sandwiches. At that point he places the meat in a bath of warm water to keep it moist and tender. When a sandwich is ordered, he cuts the corned beef very thick, across the grain, and trims away any excess fat. ("Be sure to trim the fat between the counter layers of muscle," Bob advised.)

Serve the sandwich with pickle wedges and potato chips.

Butter
2 slices light rye bread
2 slices Swiss cheese
4-6 ¼- to ½-inch-thick slices corned beef (see headnote)
Horseradish mustard to taste
¼ cup sauerkraut, drained

Butter the outside of both pieces of rye bread and lay them in a hot skillet. Place the Swiss cheese on 1 of the slices. Cook until the buttered side is crisp and golden brown, 1 to 2 minutes. Remove from the skillet. Place the sliced corned beef on the slice with the melted cheese. Top the corned beef with mustard and sauerkraut. Top with the second slice of toasted rye, cut the sandwich diagonally, and serve.

Monte Cristo

BAKER'S CAFÉ ✳ CHARLESTON, SOUTH CAROLINA

It makes sense that our recipe for the widely popular Monte Cristo sandwich comes from the worldly city of Charleston. Cooking traditions here have a complex history that includes the influence of Native Americans, settlers from the British Isles, Huguenots from France, and slaves from West Africa. In John Martin Taylor's book *Hoppin' John's Lowcountry Cooking,* he writes, "Nowhere in America did the cooking of master and slave combine so gracefully as it did in the Lowcountry kitchen." Taylor points out that in the early years of the United States, Charleston was the nation's richest city, and its well-to-do citizens imported fine wine and rare groceries from around the world.

The Monte Cristo sandwich arrived in America from France considerably later, probably sometime in the 1930s. Most historians agree that it was based on the croque monsieur, a French sandwich made of Gruyère cheese and ham that was fried in butter. It first appeared on menus and in cookbooks as the "French sandwich," and it is believed that it got its American name sometime in the 1960s in southern California.

But enough history. Let's talk about a great place called Baker's Café that serves this sandwich, along with a breakfast menu of magnificently cooked poached eggs in all sorts of combos—with country ham, with corned beef hash, with artichokes, or with crabmeat. Lunch sandwiches include chicken cordon bleu, a croissant du jour, and a vegetarian mix in pita with dilled Havarti cheese. Proprietor Kimberly Clarke reminded us that the Baker's Café Monte Cristo is always served with raspberry-rhubarb jam, a specialty of the house available by the jar at the restaurant.

1   cup heavy cream
3   large eggs
    Ground cinnamon
8   ounces smoked ham
8   ounces smoked turkey
4-6 ounces Swiss cheese
4   slices from a large white bâtard, cut diagonally
    Clarified butter for frying (recipe follows)
    Confectioners' sugar
    Raspberry-rhubarb jam (see headnote) or regular raspberry jam

Beat the cream and eggs well in a small bowl, adding cinnamon to taste. Divide the ham, turkey, and cheese between 2 slices of the bread. Top with the remaining slices, press together well, and soak the sandwiches on both sides in the cream and egg mixture.

Heat the clarified butter in a large skillet. Cook the sandwiches on both sides until the bread is golden brown and the cheese has melted. Cut in half, dust lightly with confectioners' sugar, and serve with jam on the side.

Clarified Butter

8   tablespoons (1 stick) unsalted butter

Melt the butter in a saucepan over very low heat. A white foam will form on the top; skim it off with a spoon. Remove the pan from the heat and let cool for 3 minutes. Strain the butter through cheesecloth or a fine sieve into a bowl. The liquid that seeps through is clarified butter. You will have about ⅓ cup, enough for 2 or 3 sandwiches. (The butter can be covered and refrigerated for up to 3 weeks.)

Moosey Breakfast Samich

As you might deduce from the name "samich," as well as the name of the establishment that serves it, Waldorf A'Story is a wacky sort of place. Located in a tiny town on the Bozeman Trail between Sheridan, Wyoming, and Bozeman, Montana, it is part of the Piney Creek General Store, which is a one-stop-fits-all kind of place. To quote its brochure, which is titled *Heaven is Another Story,* "This is where ya go to relax, stuff yerself, pick up some road food, a six-pack, quart of oil, and some neat stuff ya might wanna have around next time ya belly-up to the kitchen stove with good eatin' on yer mind."

That "neat stuff" ranges from Ring Dings and Twinkies to fine imported olive oil and pasta, as well as vintage wines and exotic beers. In addition to groceries, the store's shelves stock all kinds of cookware, DVDs for rent, local souvenirs, and sports equipment.

We love to ensconce ourselves at one of the mismatched tables in the dining room early in the morning, when one is privy to all sorts of conversation as locals and travelers stop in for breakfast. And while the coffee cake is great, as are the pancakes and French toast, we are particularly smitten with Waldorf A'Story's mighty breakfast sandwich, the recipe for which was provided by proprietor Patty Hoover. The goodness of this sandwich is directly proportional to the quality of the sourdough bread.

MAKES 1 SANDWICH

2   slices good sourdough bread
    Butter
2   large eggs
2   slices American cheese
4   slices cooked bacon, 1 slice fried ham, or 2 fried sausage patties
    Thin slices red onion
2   slices tomato

Butter 1 side of each slice of bread and brown it, butter side down, in a large skillet or on a griddle over low heat. While the bread browns, melt 1 tablespoon butter in a skillet and fry the eggs over medium heat, scrambling them slightly. Place the cheese on top of the eggs and cover the skillet just long enough for the cheese to melt.

Place 1 piece of the browned bread on a serving plate, browned side down. Add the cooked meat of choice and top that with the eggs and cheese. Add slices of raw onion to taste, then the tomato. Top with the remaining slice of bread. Cut the sandwich in half, using toothpicks to hold each half together. Serve immediately.

✳ Muffuletta

ALL STAR SANDWICH BAR ✳ CAMBRIDGE, MASSACHUSETTS

We nominate the muffuletta as the boldest sandwich in America. It is a Sicilian-flavored layered monument built of three major elements: fresh, firm-bodied Italian bread, top-quality cold cuts, and olive salad with a kick.

The name "muffuletta" once referred only to the bread, a chewy round loaf turned out by Italian bakeries. New Orleans grocery stores that sold the bread got the fine idea to slice it horizontally and stuff it, and the muffuletta sandwich was born. It has become a signature dish of the Big Easy but, like the po' boy, has become known nationwide.

Excellent bread and the best cold cuts are essential, but it's the olive salad that makes a muffuletta unique, and our recipe comes from one of the most amazing sandwich sources anywhere: the All Star Sandwich Bar of Cambridge, Massachusetts. Here is a small café with a huge menu of regional sandwiches from all across the U.S.A. Not pale imitations of regional sandwiches but the real thing: soft, shaved-to-order roast beef on salt-and-caraway-seed-spangled buns (from Buffalo), a swell Cuban, a classic Reuben and a Texas Reuben (the latter made with swooningly tender smoked brisket), pulled pork with coleslaw the way it's made in eastern North Carolina, ultra-hot "atomic" meat loaf, and the amazing All Star Bomb, aka the Clogger, which includes brisket, tongue, pastrami, chopped liver, Swiss cheese, and bacon!

Originally a "leftover" dish made from the pieces at the bottom of the barrel, olive salad should be briny and strong—too strong if it weren't for the flavor-cushioning effect of bread. Many groceries carry ready-made olive salad, but it is seldom as good as what you can mix up at home. All Star's version of the sandwich is billed as the Big Eazy Greazy Muffuletta because its olive salad contains plenty of oil, which will inevitably ooze and drip. It's served on slices of the sesame-seeded Italian bread called *scali,* which makes it especially messy. At home, we prefer building ours in a sturdy loaf.

Never serve a muffuletta warm. Room temperature is the rule. Serve with root beer.

MAKES 1 SANDWICH; SERVES 2 TO 4

1	large loaf fresh Italian bread (round loaf preferred)
	Olive oil (optional)
5-6	ounces thinly sliced Genoa salami
5-6	ounces thinly sliced ham
5-6	ounces mortadella
5-6	ounces thinly sliced provolone cheese
	Olive Salad (recipe follows)

Slice the loaf of bread in half horizontally and scoop out about half of the soft interior from the top and bottom.

Brush the bottom of the loaf with olive oil if you like, or with the juice from the olive salad marinade. Layer on the cold cuts and cheese. Top the cold cuts with as much olive salad as will fit without spilling out. Replace the top of the loaf.

Cut into quarters and serve.

✳ Olive Salad

MAKES 1½ CUPS, ENOUGH FOR 2 TO 3 LARGE LOAF SANDWICHES

1	cup coarsely chopped green olives
¼	cup finely diced celery
¼	cup finely diced carrot
2	teaspoons chopped garlic
2	tablespoons dried oregano
1	teaspoon freshly ground pepper
½	cup extra-virgin olive oil
2	tablespoons red wine vinegar
2	tablespoons fresh lemon juice

Thoroughly mix together all the ingredients in a medium bowl. Cover and marinate at room temperature for 12 hours. The salad will keep for several days refrigerated but gradually loses its punch.

✳ Mystery Sandwich

CHIODO'S TAVERN ✳ PITTSBURGH, PENNSYLVANIA

America lost a culinary landmark in March 2005, when Chiodo's Tavern closed its doors for good. Opened nearly six decades earlier and originally a favorite gathering place for steelworkers, it became a destination for Pittsburghers of every stripe. Hoisting a brace of brewskis at the bar or in the beer garden out back was a precious ritual. But precious don't feed the bulldog, and when eighty-seven-year-old Joe Chiodo decided it was time to call it quits, Walgreens bought the property for a drugstore.

The interior decor of Chiodo's was a trip unto itself, packed wall to ceiling with artifacts that ranged from nostalgic (a photo of the neighborhood's own "Miss Bar" riding in a convertible in a parade) to naughty (hundreds of impetuously discarded brassieres hanging from the ceiling).

You wouldn't expect good food in a place so devoted to the absorption of beer, but the Italian chicken sandwich with its red-sauce topping and the taut kielbasa with kraut were a joy, and the hamburgers were taproom classics. Chiodo's single best-known meal was an item called the Mystery Sandwich, for which no one claims ever to have secured Joe Chiodo's actual recipe. In fact, it seemed to us over several visits that the ingredients of the sandwich changed from day to day, so perhaps there never was a single recipe. In any case, the principle of the Mystery Sandwich was an archetypally Pittsburgh idea: the impossible union of a myriad of diverse ingredients, always including at least a hamburger patty, a disk or two of kielbasa and/or sliced ham, melted cheese, and sauerkraut.

After much study, we came up with a recipe that replicates the Mystery Sandwich as served at Chiodo's for fifty-seven years. This formula makes a very large sandwich, which is the way it was at Chiodo's. If you ordered a whole one, it was big enough for two. A half sandwich was a good-size meal.

Serve it with beer and many, many napkins.

1 12-inch length of French or Italian bread
Yellow mustard (optional)
2 4-ounce hamburger patties, cooked to taste
5–6 ounces kielbasa, cut into ¼-inch-thick disks
Sliced boiled ham (optional)
2 slices provolone cheese
½ cup sauerkraut, drained
¼ cup sweet onion, grilled
¼ cup sliced roasted red pepper (page 89)

Slice the bread into 2 pieces and then slice each piece in half horizontally. Smear the bottom of each half with mustard if desired. Lay the hamburger patties over the mustard. Top the burgers with the kielbasa, a slice or two of boiled ham if desired, and the provolone. Arrange the sauerkraut on the cheese, then add the onion and roasted pepper. Place the bread on top and serve.

Old-Fashioned Beer-Battered Brains

It's hard to find brains today, even in St. Louis. Common in south-city pubs in the middle of the last century, fried brain sandwiches have almost disappeared. The last time we checked, only a couple of taverns were serving them. When we first went looking, nearly every good watering hole had its version; there was even an annual citywide brain cook-off in which pub chefs competed. Among the best to be found were those served at Dieckmeyer's and the Haven, the latter billing itself as "Home of the Old Tyme Brain Sandwich."

The evening we first visited the Haven, the place was mobbed with people wearing baseball uniforms. The Haven sponsored a team, and after the game, everyone retired to the tavern to drink beer and eat brains.

The tavern's pride in serving an "old tyme" sandwich wasn't just advertising hype. Proprietor Gordon Beck explained to us that a lot of pub cooks were going to the easier, modern way of preparing the sandwich, which was to grind up the brains rather than serve them intact. The newfangled method saved time and labor because it did not require picking off the membrane, which is a painstaking process. Beck also told us that his supplier tried to sell him frozen brains. But freezing makes brains tough, and grinding makes them dense. The traditional method yields brains that are fine and fluffy, with a creamy flavor that melts over the taste buds with the tenderness of a savory marshmallow.

If you plan to make brains at home, you'll likely have to order them in advance from a specialty butcher. Mr. Beck never shared his recipe, but ours is true to the original.

2-3 whole calf's brains
1 large onion, stuck with 4 cloves
12 ounces flat beer (lager)
1½ cups all-purpose flour
2 teaspoons salt
1 teaspoon paprika
Vegetable oil for deep-frying
4-6 hard rolls, split and buttered
Optional additions: pickles, raw onions, mustard

Wash the brains well and soak them in cold water for 30 minutes. Carefully pick away any membrane, following it into the convolutions. Do your best, but realize that some membrane will remain.

Bring a pot of water to a boil. Drop the brains and the onion into the boiling water and simmer for 15 minutes. Use a slotted spoon to gently remove the brains from the pot.

Gradually stir the beer into 1 cup of the flour in a wide, shallow bowl, creating a batter. Stir in the salt and paprika.

Heat about 1 inch of oil to 375 degrees in a large, deep skillet.

Gently sever each brain into its hemispheres. Roll each half-brain in the remaining ½ cup flour, then dip it in the beer batter. Fry, turning once, until golden brown, about 5 minutes. Remove with a slotted spoon and drain well on paper towels.

Place a half-brain on the bottom half of each roll with the desired additions. Place the top half of the roll on each sandwich and serve immediately.

✳ Open-Face Hot Ham

SCHWABL'S ✳ WEST SENECA, NEW YORK

Everybody knows Schwabl's as a source of excellent beef on weck (page 18). In fact, historians surmise that it was the Schwabl family that invented it. The Schwabls had been in the restaurant trade in Buffalo since the nineteenth century, and it is believed that sometime in the 1920s one of them realized that a brightly salted sandwich would be a great way to sell more beer at their taverns.

The Schwabl family restaurant is now run by Cheryl and Gene Staychock. Cheryl was a waitress at Schwabl's for fifteen years, and she and Gene managed the place for three years before taking over. They have no intention of altering a restaurant formula that has been a favorite of Buffalonians for decades.

Years ago, when we first ate beef at Schwabl's with another couple, a waitress suggested that we not all order the same sandwich. "What about hot ham?" she said. One of us complied, and it turned out to be a delight, not so much for the ham itself, which was fine, but for the fabulous sweet-and-sour sauce that blanketed it and the zesty hot German potato salad that came alongside.

If you serve this with warm potato salad, put that on the plate before adding the sauce. The sauce should mingle with the bottom of the scoop of potato salad. Macaroni salad will work too, but it must be warm.

MAKES 4 SANDWICHES

- 8 slices soft white bread
- 1 pound boiled ham, thinly sliced (preferably by hand)
  Sweet-and-Sour Sauce (recipe follows)

Lay 2 slices bread side by side on each plate. Top the bread with one fourth of the sliced ham and ladle some of the warm sauce on top.

✳✳ Sweet-and-Sour Sauce

2   tablespoons butter
4   scallions, including a couple inches of green tops, thinly sliced
2   tablespoons all-purpose flour
¼   cup cider vinegar
1   cup apple cider, plus more if needed
¼   cup light brown sugar
1   tablespoon tomato paste
¼   teaspoon ground cloves

Melt the butter in a medium skillet and sauté the scallions until they soften, about 2 minutes. Gradually stir in the flour until it is thoroughly mixed. Add the remaining ingredients and simmer until cream-thick, about 5 minutes. Add more apple cider if the sauce gets too thick. Keep warm.

Oyster Loaf

CASAMENTO'S ✳✳ NEW ORLEANS, LOUISIANA

The oyster loaf is considered a subcategory of the po' boy, and in the sense that it's a heap of food surrounded by massive hunks of bread, that's precisely what it is. But the food is fried oysters still so warm that each one oozes sweet marine juice when bitten, which puts this big sandwich in a category all by itself.

Oyster loaves are served throughout New Orleans and the Cajun country of the South, and we've yet to find one that's bad. But for the best, loaf lovers go to Casamento's. Oysters aren't the only item of note on the menu of this spanking-clean neighborhood oyster bar, which closes for a long summer vacation when oysters aren't in season. You can also have fried fish, shrimp, and, in the spring, soft-shelled crabs, and there's even a plate of that arcane Creole Italian meal daube, which is flaps of pot roast in gravy on spaghetti noodles.

Casamento's oyster loaf is nothing short of magnificent: a dozen crackle-crusted hotties piled between two big slabs of what New Orleans cooks know as pan bread, aka Texas toast. Each single oyster is a joy, its brittle skin shattering with light pressure, giving way to a wave of melting warm, briny oyster meat across the tongue. When we asked proprietor Joe Gerdes what made his oysters so especially good, he modestly replied that his method is "too simple to call a recipe." Of course he uses freshly shucked local oysters, and he does recommend frying in lard, but the real secret is ineffable. "Everything is fried by feel and sound," he said. "It requires a lot of personal attention and experience."

In the wake of Hurricane Katrina, Casamento's reopened in November 2005, and that is a good thing. But Mr. Gerdes, who evacuated to Mississippi ahead of the storm, died the day it hit New Orleans. He was eighty years old, and so closely was he identified with the restaurant that most of the obituaries referred to him as Joseph Casamento.

- 3 large eggs
- ¼ cup heavy cream
- 1 cup fine cracker crumbs
- 1 cup yellow cornmeal
- ¼ teaspoon salt
- ¼ teaspoon cayenne pepper
- ¼ teaspoon freshly ground pepper
- 2 dozen freshly shucked oysters
  Vegetable oil for deep-frying
- 4 pieces bread cut lengthwise from a loaf of sturdy white bread, each 10 inches long and about 1½ inches thick
  Butter for spreading
  Mayonnaise or Tartar Sauce (page 39 or 51)
  Lettuce and sliced tomato (optional)

Beat the eggs and cream together in a small bowl. Place the cracker crumbs and cornmeal on separate plates.

Mix together the salt and both peppers and sprinkle the mixture over the oysters. Dip the oysters into the egg-cream mixture and then roll them in the cracker crumbs. Return them to the egg-cream mixture, then coat them with cornmeal. Set the oysters on wax paper and refrigerate.

Preheat the broiler. Heat 2 inches of oil to 375 degrees in a deep fryer or a large, deep skillet.

As the oil heats, place the bread under a broiler and cook it on both sides until light brown. When it's done, remove it from the heat and butter it.

Fry the oysters a few at a time (don't crowd the fryer) for 2 minutes, turning them once. Remove them with a slotted spoon and drain on paper towels.

Construct each sandwich by piling a dozen oysters between 2 pieces of buttered toast. Mayonnaise or tartar sauce is the preferred condiment; even lettuce and tomato are good. But be prepared: this sandwich will fall apart as you lift it from the plate.

✳ Pasty

It's debatable whether or not the pasty (rhymes with "nasty") is a sandwich, but rather than debate its nature, let's just enjoy it. It is a self-contained portable meal in a crust that was once more popular than hamburgers in the Midwest's northland. Originally brought over in the nineteenth century by Cornish settlers who came to work in Wisconsin's iron mines, pasties were designed to travel neatly inside a coat pocket, wrapped in paper. They stayed warm for hours, and if they did happen to cool, the mine worker could reheat one on the end of his shovel. A pasty requires no utensils, not even a table.

When the mines of Wisconsin were exhausted, many of the Cornish settlers moved up to the copper- and iron-rich country of "Superiorland"—northern Wisconsin and Michigan's Upper Peninsula, which had already been populated by a large number of Finnish people. The Finns adopted the Cornish pasty as their own, and now Upper Midwest pasty chauvinism is as high-spirited as the fuss chefs make over chowder in New England or barbecue in North Carolina. The question is, what is a "genuine" pasty?

Experts tend to define a Cornish pasty as the chunked-steak version, juicy inside with a tough crust for eating out of hand. Finnish pasties are more often made with a mixture of ground beef and pork that can be as dense as meat loaf. The latter invites gravy, and of course knife and fork. Further debate arises from issues such as whether the dough should be made with lard or suet and whether the filling ought to contain onions and/or rutabagas.

As we see it, such fine points are nit-picking, considering that it was Cornish custom to include any available garden vegetables or scraps of meat in a pasty. In fact, Devonshire folk used to make fun of their Cornish neighbors by saying that the devil was afraid to go to Cornwall, for fear he would be thrown into a pasty and baked.

We got this recipe from a woman we met at a church supper years ago up around Osseo, Wisconsin.

DOUGH

- 3 cups all-purpose flour
- 2 teaspoons salt
- 12 tablespoons (1½ sticks) cold unsalted butter, chopped into pea-size pieces
- ⅓ cup cold water

FILLING

- 1 pound ground chuck
- 1 pound ground pork loin
- 1½ cups chopped carrots
- 1 cup chopped onion
- 1 cup chopped potato
- 1 cup chopped rutabaga
- 1 teaspoon salt
- ½ teaspoon freshly ground pepper
- 6 teaspoons butter

PREPARE THE DOUGH: Combine the flour and salt in a large bowl and cut the butter in with your fingers or two knives until it is the size of small peas. Add just enough of the cold water, stirring it in gently with a fork, to form a ball of dough.

Knead the dough on a lightly floured surface for 3 to 5 minutes. Dust it with flour, wrap in plastic, and refrigerate for 30 to 45 minutes.

PREPARE THE FILLING: Combine all the ingredients except the butter in a large bowl and mix well.

Preheat the oven to 350 degrees.

PREPARE THE PASTIES: Divide the dough into 6 pieces, rolling each one into a 10-inch round. Place a heaping cup of filling on the top half of each dough round. Fold the dough over to form a half-moon shape. Moisten the edges and press them together to seal in the filling. Use a fork to serrate the edge, as you would with a piecrust. Cut 3 or 4 slits in the top of each one for air to escape as it bakes.

Place the pasties on a baking sheet and bake for 30 minutes. Then slip 1 teaspoon butter through one of the air slits in each pasty. Bake for 30 more minutes, or until the crust is golden brown.

Remove from the oven and let the pasties sit for 10 minutes before serving.

✳ Peanut Butter and Bacon

BECKY'S DINER ✳ PORTLAND, MAINE

Becky Rand was a woman on a mission when she opened Becky's Diner on the wharf in Portland, Maine, in 1991. "Workers from the boats and the docks had nowhere to eat!" she says with sincere astonishment. Back then, a few upscale restaurants had opened in the historic cobblestone-street district, which, although still perfumed by the fishing fleet, has since become a stylish place to shop and dine. But those restaurants charged double-digit prices and didn't want a blue-collar crowd. "Men in work clothes scared off their customers," Becky says. "I asked myself, 'Where is the nice hot meal for the all-night cabdrivers, the scallop draggers and lobstermen getting an early start, cops on the beat, and the luckless guy or gal scraping together dimes and quarters to buy a grilled cheese sandwich and a cup of coffee?'"

Successful from the beginning, Becky's is now mobbed every morning starting at four and is open every day of the year except Thanksgiving and Christmas. In addition to the cockcrow waterfront crowd she anticipated, morning habitués include white-collar power-drivers boning up on the newspapers' financial pages before their day begins, as well as breakfast connoisseurs from all over town.

The breakfast menu includes homemade muffins, French toast made from locally baked Italian bread, and "loaded" hash brown potatoes, which are mixed with peppers and onions and blanketed with melted cheese. There is a full array of the usual breakfast sandwiches and one sandwich that isn't usual at all: peanut butter and bacon. "I guess it's a breakfast sandwich," Becky said with a chuckle, but there's no reason it won't work for lunch or a midnight snack. It is rich as sin, and if you use the best ingredients, it is sheer luxury.

"The quality of the bacon is key," Becky said without equivocation, noting that bacon is by far the most popular breakfast meat in the diner. "I go through fifteen or twenty cases a week," she told us, explaining that she uses Hormel Lay-Flat strips, which she oven-bakes rather than fries. "When you bake it in the oven, it doesn't burn," Becky said. "Bake it on parchment paper, which absorbs a lot of the fat; then you don't have to drain it as much." She also gave us good peanut butter tips: buy the kind that is smooth and very dense, with a layer of oil floating on top that needs to get stirred into the peanut butter before scooping any out. (This kind of peanut butter is generally available in health-food stores and specialty markets.)

MAKES 1 SANDWICH

- 6 slices thick-cut bacon
- 2 slices sturdy bread (white or whole wheat)
- 2 tablespoons thick, smooth peanut butter (see headnote)

 Preheat the oven to 400 degrees. Line a baking sheet with parchment paper.

Lay the bacon on the baking sheet. Bake until done but not overly crisp, about 20 minutes. Drain on paper towels.

Toast the bread and spread 1 tablespoon of the peanut butter on each slice. Lay the bacon on top of the peanut butter on the bottom slice, top it with the other slice, and serve.

Peanut Butter and (Cherry) Jelly

THE CHERRY HUT ✳ **BEULAH, MICHIGAN**

It would be a sin to write a book of great American sandwiches and not include PB&J, and while probably the most traditional version is made with grape jelly, we thought we'd take the opportunity to celebrate the Cherry Hut by including its own special version of the classic lunch-box combo.

We love this fruitcentric eatery in cherry country, and to anyone who has spent time traveling Route 31 along Lake Michigan's eastern shore, the Cherry Hut has become as familiar a feature of the landscape as the cherry orchards themselves. It is known by its mascot, Cherry Jerry, "the Cheery Cherry Pie–Faced Boy" whose huge grinning likeness is perched atop a tall sign by the road north of Beulah, a pie-stop beacon in cherry country. James and Dorothy Kraker, who opened a roadside stand in 1922 to sell pies made from cherries grown on their farm, created Cherry Jerry, and since then generations of travelers have come to know and love him. In fact, the top crust of each Cherry Hut pie used to be incised with a cutter that formed Cherry Jerry's smiling features in the pastry.

The Krakers' pie-only stand evolved over the years to become a charming little restaurant with indoor tables and a short menu of farmland comfort food, including biscuit-topped chicken pie and chicken salad dotted with dried tart cherries. You can buy whole pies singly or by the tin, "tin" being the cherry-country word for a container that holds five pies, named for the large metal pail in which cherries were packed in the pre-plastic age. The Cherry Hut also sells bottles of concentrated cherry juice, which is thought to cure arthritis pain, and jars of cherry jelly, which makes the most wonderful peanut butter and jelly sandwich. The jelly (and other cherry products) can be ordered at www.cherryhut products.com or by calling 231-882-4431.

Serve this PB&J with potato chips.

MAKES 1 SANDWICH

2 slices white or whole wheat bread
1¼ teaspoons butter
1½ tablespoons Cherry Hut Cherry Jelly (see headnote)
2 tablespoons peanut butter, smooth or chunky

Spread 1 slice of bread with the butter. Spread the cherry jelly over the butter, making sure to cover the bread evenly. Spread the other slice of bread with the peanut butter, making sure no bread shows through. Combine the slices, cut the sandwich diagonally with a serrated knife, and serve.

✳ Pella Bologna

IN'T VELD MEAT MARKET ✳ PELLA, IOWA

Bologna has been a specialty of the Dutch-ancestored town of Pella since the 1860s, but you must understand that Pella bologna is unlike bologna from an ordinary supermarket. It is a coarsely ground beef sausage, well spiced and packed into natural casing, sometimes smoked over hickory, and formed into a ring about the size of a steering wheel. It is sold locally in grocery stores and butcher shops, and we always make a point of buying plenty to take home whenever we pass through.

One of the most delicious ways to enjoy this meaty treat is in a sandwich made at the In't Veld Meat Market. As the name suggests, In't Veld is mostly a butcher shop, and many of its customers come to buy steaks, sausages, and cheese to take home. But there are also a few tables for the casual lunches, which include homemade soup, hamburgers made from just-ground beef, bratwurst sausages, and house-dried beef on a bun. The basic bologna sandwich is five thick slices cut from a ring, served warm in a fresh bakery bun. Spicy mustard is essential, and the sandwich is dramatically improved by the inclusion of a few thick slices of smoky Gouda cheese, which the heat of the bologna softens into a semimelted state. To really doll it up, you can make an Iowa Reuben by adding sauerkraut or red cabbage. And if you have no genuine Pella bologna from which to make it, we recommend slices of a coarsely ground summer sausage. Pale, bland supermarket bologna simply will not suffice.

MAKES 1 SANDWICH

4-6	thick disks Pella bologna (see headnote)
1	hero roll, about 6 inches long, sliced in half horizontally
2½	slices smoked Gouda cheese
	Spicy mustard

Preheat the oven to 350 degrees.

Warm the bologna slices briefly in the oven or for a few seconds in the microwave. Arrange them on the bottom half of the roll and top them with the cheese. Spread mustard on the top half of the roll. Close the roll and eat!

✳ Perfect Ham and Cheese

BLUE WILLOW INN ✳ SOCIAL CIRCLE, GEORGIA

Located in the mansion that is said to have been the inspiration for Tara in Margaret Mitchell's *Gone With the Wind,* the Blue Willow Inn radiates Deep South hospitality. In the grand old boardinghouse spirit, it is a pay-one-price, eat-all-you-like affair with a buffet that offers a staggering array of choices. Guests graze through a room where about a half-dozen entrées and countless side dishes are arrayed in appetizing formation. Highlights include crusty fried chicken, chicken and dumplings, collard greens, fried green tomatoes, and warm fruit cobbler (plus, of course, biscuits and corn bread and relishes). Pile your plate high, dig in, then go back and pile your plate again.

There are no sandwiches at this glorious hot-supper banquet, but when we worked with proprietor Louis Van Dyke on *The Blue Willow Inn Cookbook,* he said there was at least one favorite sandwich he felt it necessary to include: ham and cheese.

A glance at the list of ingredients reveals nothing at all unusual about this familiar sandwich combo. The point here is not unique ingredients but the precise way in which the sandwich must be constructed. To quote Louis, "The important part is how the sandwich is layered to excite the taste buds." So while most sandwich recipes welcome substitutes of different brands and alterations in the formula, this one must be made exactly as described here. Serve it with potato chips.

MAKES 1 SANDWICH

- 1 tablespoon Kraft Miracle Whip
- 2 slices square sandwich bread, white or whole wheat
- 2 slices boiled ham
- 1 slice Kraft Deluxe American Cheese slices (Swiss may be substituted)
- 2 leaves iceberg lettuce
- 2 slices tomato
    Salt and freshly ground pepper
- 1½ teaspoons prepared yellow mustard

Spread Miracle Whip on each piece of bread. Place the ham on 1 piece and place the cheese on top of the ham. Add the iceberg lettuce leaves. Add the tomato. Salt and pepper the tomato to taste. Spread the mustard onto the Miracle Whip on the other slice of bread. Close the sandwich and serve.

Bonus: Summer Tomato Sandwich

MAKES 1 SANDWICH

As this book was nearing completion, Louis Van Dyke called us with an emergency. No one, he said, should be allowed to write a sandwich book without including the best sandwich on earth, available only in the summer: a tomato sandwich. "You pick that first ripe summer tomato and slice it thick into two big round pieces. You know you've got it right if the tomato juices are running down your arm as you eat it." Serve with iced tea or lemonade.

2-3 tablespoons mayonnaise
2 slices fresh white bread
2 slices ripe beefsteak tomato
Salt and freshly ground pepper

Spread the mayonnaise on both pieces of bread. Top 1 slice with the tomato and season with salt and pepper to taste. Top with the other slice of bread, cut in half, and serve.

Philly Cheesesteak

PAT'S KING OF STEAKS ✳ PHILADELPHIA, PENNSYLVANIA

Pat's invented the cheesesteak in 1930. Whether or not that claim is true, this restaurant's shaved-beef-and-cheese sandwiches on serious Italian bread have stood for over half a century as the benchmark against which other cheesesteaks are measured. The sandwich is greasy, slippery, downright ignominious, and a barrel of fun to eat. Flaps of beef are sizzled on a grill with onions and hefted into a roll, and then a trowel of melted Cheez Whiz is dripped on top. That's the classic way to have it, known to Philadelphians as a "steak, wit'." Of course it is also possible to have it wit'out: hold the onions. If you really want to dress it up, all the city's good cheesesteak emporiums offer sauce and hot peppers, and most even offer provolone cheese as an alternative to Whiz.

As we see it, the cheesesteak is a perfect combination of ingredients that transcend their modest nature to become something exceptional. For proof, we offer the fact that cheesesteaks are one of those rare local specialties that have achieved popularity almost everywhere in the United States. And while we've eaten many good ones elsewhere, they are more correct, and better, as served in Philadelphia.

Come to Pat's any time of night or day. Side your sandwich with a cup full of cheese fries (French fries smothered in more of that melted Whiz), and eat standing up on the sidewalk under harsh lights, where trucks rumble past on the street and where cheesesteak fanciers from all walks of life share in the pleasure of the signature dish of the City of Brotherly Love.

While it is possible—and extremely easy—to use frozen Steak-Ums to make cheesesteaks, your sandwiches will be much better if you get a rib-eye steak and put it in the freezer just long enough so it firms up and can be sliced paper-thin.

MAKES 2 LARGE SANDWICHES; SERVES 4

around the bone. One day after I came to Snappy Lunch, it hit me: I'll just take that bone out. But still there was a problem: the boneless chops had tough parts. That's when I realized it had to be tenderized."

Experienced pork chop eaters always order their sandwich at Snappy Lunch "all the way," which means that five separate condiments are applied: a thick slice of tomato, chopped onion, mustard, coleslaw, and Charles Dowell's special chili sauce.

"Chili is the little thing that turned out big," Mr. Dowell says with a philosophic sense of amazement. "It was chili that made the pork chop sandwich skyrocket. And the strange thing is that I learned to make it by accident. Once I started serving pork chops, I had a tomato-based chili sauce that I put on them, but customers teased me about it. 'This is not chili!' they said. 'It's chili juice.' And they were right. So I took a little of everything that was on the grill — pork chops, ham, sausage, hamburger, tenderloin; eight different kinds of meat altogether — and ran them all through the food processor with tomatoes. Now everybody wants to buy my chili by the quart."

The chili, which has the consistency of chili paste and a sweet zest to act as a foil for the creamy chop, makes Mr. Dowell's amazing sandwich unwieldy in the extreme. Served in booths or at the counter with only a wax paper wrapper to act as a holding place for fallen condiments, a Snappy Lunch pork chop sandwich requires two hands to hoist and eat. Dainty eaters use the plastic knife and fork provided to cut the sandwich in half, but even half is inevitably messy. There are no side dishes other than a bag of potato chips, and the beverage of choice is tea — iced, of course.

If you happen to have a Tenderator in your attic or come across one at a flea market, won't you please call Charles Dowell? Snappy Lunch devotees will thank you.

✳ Real Italian

COLUCCI'S HILLTOP MARKET ✳ PORTLAND, MAINE

Colucci's looks like any other corner grocery, its sign advertising "Meats—Produce—Groceries—Lottery Tickets—Ice—Deli." Inside, the shelves are stocked with a duo-cultural array of groceries that includes Twinkies and imported olive oil. We love it for the big, gnarled blueberry muffins set out each morning on the counter, for the succulent cheeseburgers made with just-ground beef, and for such démodé hot lunches as mac & cheese, beef chili, and chop suey. And it just may be the best place in Portland to get a real Italian, the submarine sandwich unique to Maine.

As proprietor Dick Colucci expertly assembled an Italian for us behind the counter of his corner store, he told us that this place has been a sandwich source since the end of World War II. Two kinds of Italians are made here: a Real Italian, which means salami and provolone topped with tomato, green pepper, pickles, onions, olives, and oil, and a Regular Italian, which features ham and American cheese, as the sandwich was originally configured just over a century ago (see page 186). Mr. Colucci advised that the big issue among Portlanders is not the lunch meat or the seasoning but the bread. "A good fresh roll is the key," he counseled, reeling off the names of bakeries known for making the long buns on which Italians are layered.

There is no place to eat inside Colucci's market; all meals and sandwiches are takeout. It occurred to us while we chomped into a Colucci's Italian off the tailgate of our car, trying valiantly to keep ingredients from spilling onto Congress Street, that Portland's version is the most anomalous variation on the theme, primarily because of the bread on which it's made. Unlike hero sandwiches of the mid-Atlantic states, Portland's Italians are made on soft white loaves similar to the kind of bun that traditionally encloses a lobster roll—but about four times the size.

For a Regular Italian, simply substitute boiled ham and American cheese for the salami and provolone.

MAKES 1 SANDWICH

1	8- to 12-inch length Italian bread (preferably soft-crusted)
4	slices cotto salami (cooked semisoft salami)
3	slices provolone cheese
1	tablespoon chopped sweet onion
3-4	very thin long slices sour pickle
3-4	slices tomato
¼	green bell pepper, cut into thin strips
4	Greek olives, pitted and cut in half
1	tablespoon olive oil
	Salt and freshly ground pepper

Slice the bread in half lengthwise and open it. Layer all the ingredients over both halves of the bread. While it is possible to try to fold the sandwich closed, expect a lot of drips and spills if you do. The most efficient way to eat an Italian is to heft the whole thing toward your mouth, keeping it as horizontal as possible as you bite.

THE ITALIAN SANDWICH
OF PORTLAND, MAINE

Although it is similar to hoagies, heroes, grinders, blimps, zeps, wedges, and sub-marines elsewhere, the Italian sandwich of Portland, Maine, has a character all its own. We remained ignorant of this regional passion for years, because the Italian tends not to be served in places people go to eat. It is a specialty of convenience stores, delis, and butcher counters in grocery stores, where it is made to order and carried out.

The origin of Portland's Italian goes back to 1903, when dockworkers convinced local baker Giovanni Amato to split his long loaves of bread and pile each open loaf with meat, cheese, and vegetables. The Italian he designed is built in such a way that once it has been constructed, it is virtually impossible to fold the loaf over into the familiar torpedo sand-wich shape. Slices of meat and cheese span both halves of the loaf, as do thick pieces of raw tomato and green bell pepper. Then the Italian is spritzed with a significant amount of olive oil, which makes even tilting it a precarious event. It is wrapped, splayed open, in plenty of butcher paper. When it is unwrapped, the inner layers of the paper are soaked with oil and freckled with black pepper.

This is one disastrously messy sandwich. The layers of salami or ham and cheese form a barrier between the soft bread below and the oily vegetables above, but once that bar-rier is breached (generally at first bite), the bread quickly absorbs what's on top, loses its ability to hold anything, and becomes just one more ingredient on the paper. By the time you near the end, the Italian no longer resembles a sandwich at all. It has become an Ital-ian cold-cut salad, laced with fluffy tufts of bread sopped with spiced oil.

✳ Roast Green Chile

LEONA'S ✳ CHIMAYO, NEW MEXICO

The village of Chimayo is off a winding road in the foothills of the Sangre de Cristos, but it isn't obscure. Generations of weavers have made its cloth a western legend, and its early nineteenth-century Santuario is a destination for religious pilgrims who believe that dirt from the earthen floor has miraculous healing powers. For four decades, hungry travelers have come to Chimayo to visit the estimable sit-down restaurant Rancho de Chimayo and to eat at the very casual Leona's Restaurante.

Situated in the shadow of the Santuario, Leona's place is all about native New Mexican food. Its fame spread because of the tortillas she makes.

The first time we drove through New Mexico, in the mid-1970s, Leona Medina-Tiede had a roadside stand on Highway 76 where she sold tortillas and chiles. At harvesttime in the fall, you could pull over and get a sandwich of just-roasted chiles wrapped in a fresh tortilla, one of the great roadside snacks of all time. If you have some freshly picked and just-roasted New Mexican chiles, hot or mild, there is absolutely no need for anything else in this sandwich. Their radiant sunshine flavor and fleshy toothsomeness stand alone. It is possible to melt some cheese onto the tortilla too.

MAKES 1 WRAP

1 New Mexican chile or other fleshy chile about 6 inches long, roasted (see page 89)
1 Flour Tortilla (recipe follows), warmed

Place the chile on the warm tortilla. Roll up and eat.

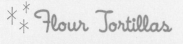 ## Flour Tortillas

MAKES 12 TORTILLAS

About 8 cups all-purpose flour
2 teaspoons baking powder
1 teaspoon salt
½ cup canola oil
3 cups warm water

Stir together the flour, baking powder, salt, and oil in a large bowl. Gradually stir in the warm water, using a fork. Add more flour if necessary so the dough is no longer sticky. Knead for 5 minutes on a lightly floured surface.

Divide the dough into 12 balls by squeezing pieces off between your thumb and forefinger. Place the balls on a lightly floured surface and cover them with a clean dish towel.

Spray a griddle with vegetable oil cooking spray (or use a nonstick griddle) and heat it to medium. (A too-hot griddle will scorch the tortillas.) Roll out the balls one at a time into 8-inch rounds. Place them, one at a time, on the griddle and cook until done, about 30 seconds per side. (The tortillas can be made up to 2 weeks ahead and refrigerated, stacked with wax paper between and covered well.)

✳ Roast Pork

LA BORINQUEÑA ✳ NEW LONDON, CONNECTICUT

Oh, how we miss La Borinqueña, a gem of a sandwich shop named for the anthem of the Commonwealth of Puerto Rico. A favorite destination along Route 1, fifteen minutes west of the Rhode Island border, La Borinqueña was a little place that offered umbrellaed picnic tables for fair-weather dining outside. It was open for a few precious years, then closed in 2005. Fans knew it as the Roast Pork Café.

The signature sandwich was a Caribbean classic: roast pork. Whole roasted shoulders were cut with scissors into variegated shreds, chunks, clods, and strips of meat that were piled inside a long hero roll, preferably with a layer of Swiss cheese and some mayonnaise, then toasted in a sandwich press that formed the potentially fall-apart sandwich into a tidy tube. The Colon family, who ran the place, would prepare a traditional Cuban as well, but it's the simplicity and intensity of roast pork, cheese, and bread that we remember.

The assembly is 1-2-3, and if you have a sandwich press, so much the better, but the key part here is the juice-dripping pork shoulder.

MAKES 1 SANDWICH

1   8- to 12-inch length Cuban (or French) bread
    Mayonnaise
1   cup (about 8 ounces) shredded Roast Pork (recipe follows)
2   slices Swiss cheese
    Butter if cooking sandwich in a skillet

Slice the bread lengthwise down the middle. Spread both sides with mayonnaise to taste. Fill with the pork and cheese. Press the two halves together.

If you have a sandwich press, cook the sandwich until the outside is toasty crisp and the cheese has melted. Otherwise, melt some butter in a skillet over medium heat. Place the sandwich in the skillet and weigh it down with another heavy skillet. Turn the sandwich once to toast both sides. Serve hot.

Roast Pork

- 1 6-pound boneless pork shoulder (not pork loin, which is too lean)
- 2 tablespoons salt
- 6 garlic cloves
- 1 teaspoon freshly ground pepper
- ½ teaspoon dried oregano
- ¼ cup olive oil
- 1 teaspoon red wine vinegar

Rinse the pork and pat it dry. Place it on a rack in a roasting pan. Use a knife to pull the skin away (but not entirely off), and remove as much of the fat as possible. Rub the salt into the meat. Use the knife to make 6 deep incisions in the meat.

Using a mortar and pestle or a mini food processor, grind together the garlic, pepper, oregano, and 1 tablespoon of the olive oil to form a thick paste. Press the paste into the incisions in the meat.

Mix the vinegar with the remaining 3 tablespoons olive oil and rub this all over the meat and the skin. Cover and refrigerate for at least 6 hours or overnight. Bring to room temperature before roasting.

Preheat the oven to 300 degrees.

Roast the shoulder skin side up, basting it occasionally with the marinade, until an instant-read thermometer registers 185 degrees, 3 to 4 hours.

Remove the roast from the oven and let it stand for 30 to 45 minutes. Use scissors (or your hands) to separate it into shreds that are a little bit bigger than bite-size.

⚹ Rodger's Big Picnic (Asparagus and Mushroom)

ZINGERMAN'S DELI *⚹* **ANN ARBOR, MICHIGAN**

While many people think of Michigan as the place where automobiles are made, it also happens to be serious farm country, a source of superb vegetables and fruits from spring berries through autumn apples. One of the best places to get to know Michigan's bounty is the Ann Arbor Farmers' Market on Detroit Street, open every Saturday throughout the year and on Wednesdays, too, from May through December. Here farmers sell maple syrup, jams and jellies, eggs, and cheese in addition to produce, and local craftsmen display pottery, furniture, jewelry, and hand-knit apparel.

Rodger's Big Picnic, a vegetarian sandwich, is Zingerman's Deli's ode to the market. Zingerman's started as a twenty-seat eatery near the market and has since become a huge culinary emporium where great sandwiches are part of the international menu.

Specifically, this sandwich depends on good asparagus, preferably Michigan asparagus. Zingerman's co-owner Ari Weinzweig says, "I love roasting asparagus, because it concentrates the flavors so nicely." Ari says this is one of the best vegetarian sandwich combos, because of the intensity of the asparagus, the richness of the cheddar, and the sharpness of the Dijon mustard. The sandwich was named for Rodger Bowser, the chef at the deli.

4 ounces asparagus (4-5 medium spears)
   Olive oil
   Sea salt
2 ounces (1 large) portobello mushroom
2 slices country bread
2 tablespoons smooth Dijon mustard, plus more to taste
2 thick slices Grafton cheddar cheese (sharp or mild, to taste)

Preheat the oven to 450 degrees.

Place the asparagus in a single layer in a baking pan and toss it lightly with a little olive oil and sea salt. Roast, turning it occasionally, for 15 to 20 minutes, or until the asparagus is light golden and tender in the middle. Set it aside and keep it warm.

Preheat a grill or the broiler.

Lightly brush the top and bottom of the mushroom with olive oil. Grill or broil for 3 to 4 minutes on each side.

Spread each slice of bread to the edge with a little over 1 tablespoon of the mustard. Top 1 slice with the roasted asparagus, grilled mushroom, and cheddar. Close the sandwich and lightly brush the outside of the bread with olive oil.

Place the sandwich in a hot skillet and grill each side for 2 to 4 minutes, or until the bread is golden brown—just long enough to grill the bread without melting the cheese. Cut in half diagonally and serve.

San Diego's Best Tuna Melt

THE COTTAGE ✳ LA JOLLA, CALIFORNIA

Nothing served on the cheerful al fresco patio of the Cottage is humdrum. Even the bread for its tuna melt is special: good California sourdough that has been infused with the assertive flavor of Parmesan cheese. This plays off the cheddar and makes the sandwich sing.

A truly best tuna melt depends also on top-quality tuna fish. Since this sandwich is unlike the typical tuna melt based on tuna salad, the flavor of the fish itself is crucial. When we are feeling flush, we go for the imported Italian stuff, packed in olive oil.

Like most tuna melts, this one is best served open-face, and while it can be hoisted from the plate by hand, a knife and fork are appreciated by most people who tackle one.

MAKES 8 OPEN-FACE SANDWICHES; SERVES 4

- 4 tablespoons (½ stick) butter, softened
- 8 tablespoons grated Parmesan cheese
- 8 slices sourdough bread
- 8 strips bacon
- 4 tablespoons mayonnaise
- 2⅔ cups tuna fish, preferably packed in olive oil, drained
- 8 slices cheddar cheese
- 2 large tomatoes, each cut into 4 thick slices

Preheat the broiler.

Combine the butter with the Parmesan in a small bowl. Mix well and spread the mixture on each slice of bread. Put the bread under the broiler for 1 to 2 minutes, or until the cheese turns golden brown; watch carefully so it doesn't burn. Remove from the heat and let cool.

Fry the bacon until crisp. Drain and set it aside.

Place a slice of bread on a plate, cheese side down. Spread ½ tablespoon of the mayonnaise on the untoasted side of the bread. Spread with ⅓ cup tuna fish. Place a strip of bacon on top and a slice of cheddar atop the bacon. Repeat with the remaining slices of bread.

Place the sandwich halves on a baking sheet and broil until the cheddar is melted, being careful that it doesn't burn. Remove from the broiler and top each half with a tomato slice. Serve hot, allotting 2 halves per person.

Santa Maria Tri-Tip

THE COTTAGE ✳✳ LA JOLLA, CALIFORNIA

Starting every Friday in Santa Maria, California, an hour north of Santa Barbara, gusts of aromatic smoke begin to blow across the city's broad avenues and through public parking lots as dozens of local pit men fire up their portable open cookers and marshal big chunks of tri-tip steak in rows on their grates.

All weekend, from midday until after dusk, beef sizzles in the open air; when its crust glistens black, a steak is forked off and sliced thick. The heavy flaps of beef are rimmed with pepper and garlic and infused with the taste of fire. It is easy meat to slice, but the rosy fibers offer some nice resistance to the tooth and surrender a lush bouquet of flavor. This fabulous food is the centerpiece of a feast that is hallowed on the central California coast, the Santa Maria–style barbecue.

That is the inspiration for a sensational sandwich served by our favorite restaurant down La Jolla way, the Cottage.

Cooking the beef for tri-tip sandwiches and making the pico de gallo and garlic aïoli is some trouble, but for a special-occasion party attended by enthusiastic carnivores, there are few treats more pleasing. The spice rub, pico de gallo, and aïoli can all be made in advance. And if you can't get tri-tip at your local butcher shop, you can substitute a good grilling steak of your choice.

3 pounds tri-tip steak (see headnote)
¼ cup olive oil
½ cup Santa Maria Spice Rub (recipe follows)
8 submarine rolls
1 cup Garlic Aïoli (recipe follows)
Pico de Gallo (recipe follows)

Heat a barbecue grill.

Brush the steak with olive oil. Rub some of the spice mixture on both sides of the meat. Grill the steak to the desired doneness (20 to 25 minutes for medium-rare), then slice it against the grain into thin slices.

Cut the rolls in half horizontally and remove some of the bread from the bottom halves to make room for the pico de gallo. Spread 1 tablespoon garlic aïoli on the top and bottom half of each roll. Fill the bottom half of each roll with ¼ cup pico de gallo. Layer the slices of steak on the bottom halves, dividing them evenly. Cap with the top halves of the bread and serve.

Santa Maria Spice Rub

MAKES ABOUT 2 CUPS

¼ cup salt
¼ cup sugar
¼ cup dark brown sugar
¼ cup ground cumin
¼ cup chili powder
¼ cup freshly ground pepper
2 tablespoons cayenne pepper
½ cup paprika

Mix everything together in a small bowl. The spice rub can be stored in an airtight container for up to 6 months.

Garlic Aïoli

MAKES 2 CUPS

½ cup chopped fresh parsley
3 tablespoons minced garlic
1½ tablespoons fresh lemon juice
¾ teaspoon dried tarragon
¾ teaspoon freshly ground pepper
½ cup olive oil
1½ cups mayonnaise

Mix together the parsley, garlic, lemon juice, tarragon, and pepper in a medium bowl. Pour this into a blender and, with the motor running, slowly add the olive oil. Pour the mixture back into the bowl and fold in the mayonnaise. Refrigerate if not using immediately.

Tightly covered and refrigerated, the aïoli will keep for up to 2 weeks.

Pico de Gallo

MAKES ABOUT 2 CUPS

- 1 cup diced Roma tomatoes
- ½ cup chopped red onion
- ½ jalapeño pepper, seeded and diced
- 1 garlic clove, minced
- ¼ cup chopped fresh cilantro
- 1 tablespoon red wine vinegar
- 1 tablespoon fresh lime juice
- ½ teaspoon dried oregano
  Salt and freshly ground pepper, to taste

Mix together all the ingredients in a small bowl. The salsa will keep, covered and refrigerated, for up to 2 days.

Sardines on Rye

THE PINE CLUB ✳ DAYTON, OHIO

The Pine Club is a definitive Midwest supper club: it is open only for dinner, it has a seriously wonderful bar that spans the center of the restaurant, it has no party rooms, it has no daily specials, it takes no reservations, and the limited menu doesn't even list dessert. Bring cash, because credit cards are not accepted. Here is an eat-place honed to the essentials.

Most people think of the Pine Club as a meat-eater's destination, and rightfully so. The steaks and veal chops are world-class, and the hamburgers—freshly ground from a blend of prime beef and dry-aged lamb—are succulence incarnate. But there's another item that must not be overlooked: the sardines on rye sandwich. Pine Club president David Hulme told us it has been on the menu since the restaurant opened in 1947, describing it as "a simple preparation of a great product for sardine lovers only." Even if you are not a sardine lover, this sandwich just might make you one, especially if you use really good olive-oil-packed sardines. The Pine Club uses Portuguese sardines, caught between May and November, grilled, then packed in clear, heavy olive oil.

Mr. Hulme reminded us that there is in fact no fish called a sardine. "The term 'sardine' refers to various small fish that are all members of the herring family," he said. "The sardine was first canned at the beginning of the nineteenth century, when Napoleon realized that there was a need to preserve food. Sardines are named after the Mediterranean island of Sardinia, where they have been extremely popular for hundreds of years."

4   large slices dark rye bread
    Grainy mustard
1   4-ounce can oil-packed sardines, drained
4   thin slices Spanish onion
    Iceberg lettuce leaves

Spread 2 of the slices of bread with mustard. Lay half the sardines on each of these slices. Place the onion on top of the sardines, then add the lettuce and top with the remaining slices of bread. Serve.

Sep Pep Pizza

HOT TRUCK ✳ ITHACA, NEW YORK

Even those Cornell University students with scant aptitude for language quickly become fluent in the idiom of Hot Truck. Spoken mostly late at night, Hot Truck is a short-order patois used to describe the sandwiches served from the side of an eponymous delivery van that is parked at the edge of West Campus. The food, as well as the language of the Hot Truck, is called Hot Truck, meaning that when the craving strikes anytime after 10 P.M., which is when the van plugs into the lamppost for the juice to power its ovens, the hungry Cornellian will never say, "Let's go to the Hot Truck and eat sandwiches." The proper construction is "Let's eat Hot Truck."

Hot Truck—the food—is a hot pizza submarine sandwich baked open-face on a length of French bread, then folded over like the familiar hero. It is served in configurations with names that can seem as obscure as Navajo. The suicide, or SUI (pronounced "sooey," like the pig call), got its name because it is piled with a suicidal quantity of ground sausage, pepperoni, and mushrooms on a bed of tomato sauce under a mound of melted mozzarella.

Hot Truck—the business—began as a pizza truck from which its owner, Bob Petrillose, sold whole pies and slices. Bob was unhappy because most of the slices he sold were reheated, sometimes hours old and soggy. He solved the problem by creating a pizza sub, called Poor Man's Pizza (PMP in Hot Truck lingo), which was made to order, served crisp and piping hot. His invention became a campus sensation, and Ithaca folklore holds that one of the students who assisted Petrillose took the idea to Stouffer's, begetting French Bread Pizza.

When we asked the Smith family, who bought Hot Truck in 2000, for a recipe, they suggested the Sep Pep, which is a WGC with mushrooms and pepperoni. A WGC is wet garlic with cheese. In Hot Truck lingo, "wet" means tomato sauce.

2   24-inch-long loaves French bread
    Garlic Sauce (recipe follows)
    Pizza Sauce (recipe follows)
3   cups sliced mushrooms
3   cups shredded mozzarella cheese
2   cups sliced pepperoni
1   tablespoon dried oregano

Preheat the oven to 375 degrees.

Cut the French bread loaves in half and slice them completely open horizontally. (This will allow the bread to lie flat in the oven to prevent burning edges.) Place the pieces of bread on a baking sheet.

Use a brush to spread the garlic sauce on all 4 pieces of bread.

Use a ladle or spoon to spread the pizza sauce on all 4 pieces of bread, being sure to cover out to the edges (to prevent burning).

Spread ¾ cup mushrooms across each bottom half of the bread. Spread ¾ cup mozzarella over the mushrooms. Spread ½ cup (about 20 slices) pepperoni across the mozzarella. Sprinkle with some oregano.

Bake until the cheese is melted and the French bread is golden brown, 8 to 10 minutes. Lay the top halves of the French bread on the bottom halves to make sandwiches.

Garlic Sauce

- 10 tablespoons (1 stick plus 2 tablespoons) margarine or butter
- 1 tablespoon garlic powder

In a medium bowl, microwave the margarine for about 3 minutes, or until completely melted. Add the garlic powder and mix thoroughly. (Alternatively, melt the margarine in a small saucepan on the stovetop and stir in the garlic powder.)

Pizza Sauce

- 1 cup tomato juice
- 2 cups store-bought pizza sauce with basil
- 1 tablespoon garlic powder
- ½ tablespoon salt

Mix together all the ingredients in a medium bowl.

*⁎⁎ Sheboygan Brat

CHARCOAL INN *⁎⁎ SHEBOYGAN, WISCONSIN

"Brat" (rhymes with "hot") is short for bratwurst, and the place to eat one is Sheboygan, Wisconsin. When you drive through town on a clear summer evening, you see a haze from backyard cookouts wafting up into the blue sky above Lake Michigan. Brats are the city's pride, and charcoal cooking is so prevalent that pork chops, hamburgers, and steaks cooked over coals are known hereabouts as Sheboygan-style foods. The first time we visited the Charcoal Inn and inquired of the waitress if her brats were cooked over coals, she replied, "My dears, everything we make is charcoaled except the BLTs and the egg salad."

Sheboygan brats are brightly spiced link sausages, 4 to 6 inches long, made of pork or a combination of beef and pork. Some of the town's butchers have developed chicken brats and turkey brats as alternatives, and during deer season, venison brats are popular in hunters' homes. Whatever they are made from, Sheboygan brats share a unique flavor that usually comes from being immersed in beer at some point during their preparation. Some bratmeisters boil the sausages in a brew of pilsner and onions and merely finish them over hot coals; others steep them cold, then do all their cooking on the grill. Chuck Miesfeld, a third-generation sausage maker, says beer is what you drink with the sausages, not what you cook them in.

It is impossible to think of a brat presented in any way other than as the heart of a hard-roll sandwich. In fact, it is almost impossible to think of *one*, for the vast majority of brats are eaten two to a sandwich. "Double brat, with the works" is the Sheboyganite's call to glory.

The Sheboygan hard roll at the Charcoal Inn is tender inside to sop up large amounts of butter and has a supple, leathery texture that makes it easy to grip, transforming it into a kind of mitt for holding on to all its ingredients. A good hard roll can stand in. But there is no substitute for an authentic Sheboygan brat, which can be ordered from Miesfeld's Market: 920-565-6328 or www.miesfeldsmarket.com.

MAKES 1 SANDWICH

Butter

2 Miesfeld's Sheboygan brats (see headnote)

1 hard roll, split in half

Choice of additions, including pickles, German mustard, onions, and/or sauerkraut

Preheat a charcoal grill or melt plenty of butter in a skillet.

Cook the brats, either whole or split, on the grill or in the skillet, turning them, for 20 to 25 minutes, or until firm to the touch.

Toast the roll on the grill or in the skillet. Butter the roll generously. Insert the brats. Top with your additions of choice and serve.

Shrimpburger

EDISTO BEACH CAFÉ ✳ **EDISTO ISLAND, SOUTH CAROLINA**

"There are not many places left like Edisto," Charlie White told us. Charlie is the proprietor of the Edisto Beach Café by the ocean, adjacent to the Piggly Wiggly grocery store. He was understating Edisto's uniqueness. Because the barrier island's palmetto-shaded beach is the nesting place for endangered loggerhead turtles from May through autumn, disruptive activities are perforce restrained: no toys or picnic gear may be left on the sand at night, terrapin harassment is punishable by a $20,000 fine, and waterfront residents must keep lights off or drapes drawn after dark so the shoreline remains serene enough for egg-laying. "We're off the beaten path and we like it that way," Charlie declared, reminding us that the island doesn't have a single fast-food franchise nor a traffic light. The only theme-park attraction on the seaward side of the intracoastal waterway is a modest serpentarium.

We went to this sea-air paradise to eat at the Old Post Office (see page 131), but we were also smitten by Charlie White's friendly little beachside establishment and its delicious shrimpburger. We never got its history but assume its name derives from the simple reason that it is served on a hamburger bun. In fact, what's inside the bun bears no resemblance to a hamburger. It is a pile of glistening shrimp laced with caramelized onions.

It's obvious that the goodness of this dish depends on the quality of its shrimp. Size matters, too. You don't want colossal shrimp (less than 10 per pound), but neither do you want the smaller ones (known as large). You want jumbos or extra-large, meaning 16 per pound. A nice, sweet Vidalia onion also adds immensely to a shrimpburger's appeal. On Edisto Island, everybody knows the best place to get sweet Vidalias is George & Pink's vegetable stand down Eddingsville Beach Road.

MAKES 3 SANDWICHES

1 pound shell-on jumbo (16 count) shrimp
¼ cup olive oil
¼ cup clarified butter (see page 152)
1 Vidalia onion, thinly sliced
 Salt and freshly ground pepper
3 hamburger buns
 Lemon wedges (optional)

Butterfly the shrimp by slicing them lengthwise almost all the way through, but leave the shells on.

Heat the olive oil and clarified butter in a large, heavy skillet over medium heat. Add the onion and salt and pepper to taste and cook, stirring, until the onion softens and turns golden brown, 10 to 15 minutes. Use a slotted spoon or fork to transfer the onion to a large bowl.

Turn the heat under the skillet to high. Add the shrimp and cook for 2 minutes on each side. Remove the shrimp from the pan. Let the shrimp cool slightly and then remove the shells, adding the peeled shrimp to the bowl with the cooked onion. (Or use gloves to peel the shrimp while they are still hot.) Mix together. Put about 5 shrimp on each bun, with an equal amount of caramelized onion, and serve hot, with a squeeze of lemon if desired.

Sloppy Joe

SLOPPY JOE'S ✳ KEY WEST, FLORIDA

With the exception of some parts of New Jersey, where "sloppy Joe" refers to a cold-cut dagwood with coleslaw and Russian dressing on deli rye, most of America knows this sandwich as some sort of ground meat (most commonly beef) mixed with a modestly spiced tomato sauce and served on a hamburger bun. Sloppy Joe is everywhere. It is a favorite of institutional cooks because it is easy to make in large quantities. Pinchpennies like it because they can use cheap beef and even stretch it out by including rice or small-shaped pasta, thus verging on the Yankee penny-saver, American chop suey. You can even buy it in a can, with the brand name Manwich.

No documentary evidence exists about the origin of the sloppy Joe sandwich, other than the claim on the menu of Sloppy Joe's restaurant in Key West that it serves "the original Sloppy Joe Sandwich [that] made us and Key West famous." Okay, we'll accept that boast, because Sloppy Joe's really is a part of Key West history. A bar operated by Joe Russell under government radar during Prohibition, it was where Ernest Hemingway is said to have gone for many bottles of illegal Scotch. The day Prohibition was repealed, the speakeasy opened as the Blind Pig. It then became the Silver Slipper when a dance floor was added, and the restaurant's version of history is that Hemingway convinced Russell to change the name to Sloppy Joe's after one of Papa's favorite places in Havana. It moved to its present location in 1937 and has since become one of the big tourist attractions on Duval Street. You can not only eat and drink; you can buy T-shirts and beer mugs, refrigerator magnets and shot glasses. And every year during the weeklong Hemingway Days celebration (which began in this bar in 1981), Sloppy Joe's hosts a Papa look-alike contest judged by members of the author's family.

One of the fun things about making a sloppy Joe is that just about anything goes. Substitute turkey or tofu for the beef, make it hotter, or cut out the chili powder altogether. Use less tomato sauce if you like it less sloppy, or even substitute a great barbecue sauce for half of the tomato sauce (in which case, it's probably best to reduce or eliminate other spices). Here's a good template from which to develop your own recipe.

1 tablespoon vegetable oil
1 pound ground chuck
2/3 cup chopped onion
1/2 cup chopped green bell pepper
1 15-ounce can tomato sauce
2 tablespoons quick-cooking oatmeal
2 teaspoons Worcestershire sauce
1/2-1 teaspoon chili powder
1/4 teaspoon freshly ground pepper
   Hot sauce, Tabasco sauce, or cayenne pepper, to taste
8 hamburger buns, warmed

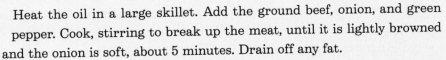

Heat the oil in a large skillet. Add the ground beef, onion, and green pepper. Cook, stirring to break up the meat, until it is lightly browned and the onion is soft, about 5 minutes. Drain off any fat.

Add the remaining ingredients (except the buns!) and simmer, uncovered, for 25 minutes, until the mixture is only a little sloppy, not soupy.

Spoon about 1/2 cup sloppy Joe into each bun and serve.

✳ Smoked Cajun Shrimp Salad

HOOVER'S COOKING ✳ **AUSTIN, TEXAS**

Hoover's Cooking is a meat-and-three kind of place, where the custom is to serve each entrée with three side dishes, including such soulful stalwarts as mashed potatoes, macaroni and cheese, black-eyed peas, porky mustard greens, crisp-fried okra, and jalapeño-accented creamed spinach. The meats at Hoover's are wonderful—Hoover's has its own smokehouse, which perfumes the parking lot with the aroma of pork ribs, sausage from nearby Elgin, highly spiced Jamaican jerk chicken, and lesser-spiced (but nonetheless delicious) barbecued chicken. Among the nonsmoked entrées are a superb chicken-fried steak, meat loaf, and catfish.

In addition to the hot meals, Hoover's offers a small array of stupendously good sandwiches. When we asked the owner, Hoover Alexander, for a choice sandwich recipe, he suggested Smoked Cajun Shrimp Salad.

At the restaurant, the shrimp is cooked in the smokehouse. But if you don't have a smokehouse or even a backyard smoker of your own, it is perfectly possible to make the shrimp for this recipe on any charcoal grill.

MAKES 2 EXTRA-LARGE SANDWICHES

SHRIMP

2½	pounds shrimp (20-24 count), peeled and deveined
¼	cup Italian salad dressing
1	tablespoon Cajun seasoning

DRESSING

5-6	ounces cream cheese
½	cup chopped celery
¼	cup chopped scallions
1	tablespoon fresh lemon juice
1	tablespoon chopped fresh parsley
½	cup mayonnaise
1½	teaspoons Cajun seasoning
2	12-inch-long submarine rolls

PREPARE THE SHRIMP: Start a barbecue grill. Get the briquettes red-hot and scoot them over to one side of the grill. Put a bunch of hickory chunks all around the hot coals.

Combine the shrimp, salad dressing, and Cajun seasoning in a bowl; toss to mix. Place the shrimp on an iron pan or on thick layers of aluminum foil and set it on the far end of the grill, away from the coals. Then cover the grill and let the smoke from the hickory (rather than direct heat from the coals) cook them. The internal temperature of the covered grill should be no more than 230 degrees. Slow-smoke the shrimp for 30 to 45 minutes, or until they are cooked through.

PREPARE THE DRESSING: Soften the cream cheese by zapping it in the microwave for 30 seconds, then stirring, then zapping again. Continue until the cheese is creamy-soft. Combine the cheese with the remaining ingredients in a large bowl.

Combine the shrimp with the dressing. Refrigerate the shrimp salad until cold, or spread it out on a baking sheet and put it in the freezer long enough to quick-cool it. (Do not freeze!)

Split the submarine rolls horizontally, divide the shrimp salad between them, and serve.

Smoked Salmon Spread

SMOKE HOUSE RESTAURANT ✳ FORKS, WASHINGTON

It was 1978 when we came across Slathar's Smoke House Restaurant along Highway 101 in Forks, Washington, near Olympic National Park. It has changed hands since then, but it's still the same destination restaurant for travelers in search of hearty meals of steak, prime rib, and—the house specialty—alderwood-smoked salmon. In a cedar-paneled space that used to be a common coffee shop, with booths up front and tables in back, families come to enjoy not only surf-and-turf but also lovely hamburgers with French fries and excellent milk shakes.

The smokehouse is part of the restaurant operation and the source of what is known as cold-smoked salmon. That means that rather than getting broiled over a fire, the fish is hung for hours to absorb smoke from smoldering alderwood. The result is a piece of salmon that is very juicy and vividly flavored.

Back in the late 1970s, shortly after Stephen Torgesen took over the smokehouse and salmon cannery that had been around for years, we wangled a handful of recipes from him. He explained that while he, of course, used fresh-smoked salmon in the restaurant, his recipes called for canned salmon, which anyone can buy in almost any supermarket. "Vitamin D, the sunshine vitamin, is abundant in canned salmon," he reminded us. So don't feel bad about using canned in this recipe—but if you have freshly smoked salmon, that is even better.

Smoked salmon spread is great between slices of toasted sourdough bread, but it also serves well as an hors d'oeuvre on crackers or stuffed into a stalk of celery or a cherry tomato.

MAKES 2 SANDWICHES

1 7-ounce can smoked salmon, drained
1/3 cup finely chopped celery
1/3 cup finely chopped onion
1 teaspoon fresh lemon juice
1/3 cup mayonnaise
1 tablespoon honey mustard
1 tablespoon Dijon mustard or other hot mustard with bite
 Salt and freshly ground pepper
4 thick, large slices bread, preferably sourdough, toasted
 Lettuce and tomato (optional)

Mix together the salmon, celery, onion, lemon juice, mayonnaise, and mustards; do not pulverize the mixture. Add salt and pepper to taste. Refrigerate until cold.

Spread the salmon mixture on 2 slices of the toast, add lettuce and tomato if desired, and top with the remaining slices of toast. Cut in half and serve.

*✳ Souvlaki

Souvlaki is a star attraction at Greek-run diners throughout the Northeast, where it is usually served on a plate with a knife and fork. A more traditional approach is to wrap the pita bread around the ingredients and eat it out of hand, but the essential sloppiness of the ingredients makes that a significant challenge. The souvlaki made by Romano Famous Pizza in the general vicinity of Astoria, in Queens, is exemplary.

Souvlaki from a pizza place? That's New York, and that is Astoria in particular, for here are all kinds of Greek foods at all levels and from some of the most unlikely sources. Romano's pizza is also great and its Caesar salad superlative. You'll be sorely disappointed if you expect welcoming smiles and pampering, but for us, the attitude is all part of the Queens cheap-eats experience.

MAKES 4 SOUVLAKI

¼ cup olive oil
2 garlic cloves, minced
2 teaspoons dried oregano
1 teaspoon freshly ground pepper
½ teaspoon salt
1 pound boneless, skinless chicken, cut into bite-size cubes
2 green bell peppers, seeded and cut into bite-size pieces
1 red onion, cut into bite-size chunks
2 tomatoes, cut into bite-size chunks
4 extra-large pita breads, warmed
   Tzatziki Sauce (recipe follows)

You will need eight metal or wooden skewers. If using wooden skewers, soak them in water for 1 hour.

Mix the olive oil, garlic, oregano, pepper, and salt in a small bowl.

Alternate the chicken cubes with the bell peppers, onion, and tomatoes on the skewers and place the skewers in a shallow pan. Pour the marinade over them, cover, and refrigerate for 4 hours, turning the skewers occasionally to marinate on all sides.

Preheat a grill or the broiler.

Grill or broil the souvlaki, turning the skewers so the meat cooks evenly, until the meat is charred at its edges and cooked through inside, 6 to 8 minutes total.

Set each pita bread on a plate and place the contents of two skewers on each pita. Serve the Tzatziki Sauce on the side. The pitas can be folded and lifted from the plate, but we recommend using a knife and fork.

Tzatziki Sauce

MAKES ABOUT 2 CUPS

1 cup peeled, seeded, finely chopped cucumber
2 garlic cloves, minced
1/4 teaspoon salt
1/4 teaspoon freshly ground pepper
1 cup plain yogurt (not low-fat or nonfat)
Juice of 1/2 lemon

Combine all the ingredients in a small bowl, cover, and refrigerate.

⁑ Spiedies

SHARKEY'S TAVERN ⁑ BINGHAMTON, NEW YORK

If you once lived around Binghamton, New York, and moved away, you probably miss spiedies something awful. A spiedie is a Broome County craving with ethnic antecedents (the Italian *spiedini*) but no American cognate. Its essential element is a skewer of long-marinated hunks of lamb (sometimes pork, chicken, or beef) cooked to a crisp over charcoal.

Sharkey's Tavern on Glenwood Avenue in Binghamton is our favorite place to eat spiedies. It's an old-fashioned place where generations come for supper and to enjoy each other's company. "We encourage people to bring their children," Larry Sharak told us. "After all, we all grew up here, my whole family." Although children are welcome, Larry likes to point out that there is no children's menu. "Kids around here learn to eat spiedies at an early age."

The Sharak family recipe for spiedies is top-secret, but several years ago we developed a spiedie marinade that is close to the tavern's. Although any type of grill works (Larry told us some people fry their spiedies in a pan), a hot charcoal flame gives the chunks of meat a crustiness that's hard to beat.

MAKES ENOUGH MEAT FOR 12 SANDWICHES; SERVES 6

MARINADE

- ¾ cup olive oil
- ½ cup dry red wine
- ½ cup red wine vinegar
- 4 garlic cloves, minced
- 1 teaspoon freshly ground pepper
- 1 teaspoon dried thyme
- ½ teaspoon ground allspice
- 2 fresh mint leaves, crushed
- 1 bunch fresh parsley, finely chopped (²/₃ cup)

- 2 pounds lean boneless lamb, cut into 1-inch cubes
- 12 large slices sturdy Italian bread

MAKE THE MARINADE: Combine all the marinade ingredients in a large bowl.

Add the lamb, toss to coat, and transfer the lamb and marinade to a sealable plastic bag. Marinate, refrigerated, for a full 24 hours, turning the bag occasionally so the meat soaks evenly.

MAKE THE SPIEDIES: Heat a barbecue grill.

Thread the lamb chunks on eight to ten metal skewers and grill them over hot coals until cooked to medium, turning them so they cook evenly, about 8 minutes altogether.

Serve the meat on the skewers and use the slices of bread to pull off 2 or 3 chunks at a time.

✳ Spiedini of Beef

LOUIE'S BACKYARD ✳ **KEY WEST, FLORIDA**

Spiedini is the Italian word for all kinds of skewered or toothpicked chunks of meat. At Louie's Backyard in Key West, spiedini are meatballs threaded on skewers along with breaded mozzarella cubes, all cooked on a charcoal grill and served over pomodoro sauce and couscous. Chef Doug Shook told us that the same ingredients, minus the couscous, make a terrific sandwich. Piled into a sturdy length of Italian bread, this is the most extremely deluxe variation of a meatball sub you will ever meet.

MAKES 6 SANDWICHES

	Meatballs (recipe follows)
	Breaded Mozzarella Cubes (recipe follows)
	Olive oil
6	8-inch grinder rolls
	Pomodoro Sauce (recipe follows)

Soak six wooden skewers in water for 1 hour.

Heat a barbecue grill.

Thread the meatballs and breaded mozzarella cubes, alternating, onto the skewers. Brush the meatballs and cheese with olive oil and grill them over medium-hot charcoal for 10 to 12 minutes, turning three or four times, until the cheese browns and the meatballs are cooked through.

Slice the rolls in half horizontally and scoop out some of their interior to make room for the ingredients. Place 4 meatballs and 3 mozzarella cubes inside each roll. Top with the warm tomato sauce and serve.

 Meatballs

    1   pound ground beef
    2   large eggs
  ½   cup grated pecorino Romano cheese
  ½   cup unseasoned dried bread crumbs
    2   tablespoons chopped garlic
    1   teaspoon sea salt
  ½   teaspoon freshly ground pepper

Combine all the ingredients in a large bowl and mix them together with your hands or a wooden spoon. Form the mixture into 24 balls and set them in the refrigerator, covered with plastic wrap. These can be made up to 1 day ahead.

Breaded Mozzarella Cubes

    2   large eggs
    1   cup all-purpose flour
1½   cups unseasoned dried bread crumbs
    1   tablespoon crushed red pepper flakes
    1   pound mozzarella cheese, preferably fresh, cut into 18 cubes

Beat the eggs in a small bowl.

Spread the flour out on a plate. Mix together the bread crumbs and crushed red pepper in a wide, shallow plate. Dip each mozzarella cube first in the flour, then in the egg, then in the crumb mixture.

✳ Pomodoro Sauce

MAKES ENOUGH FOR 6 SANDWICHES

- 6 large ripe tomatoes
- ½ cup olive oil
- 1 tablespoon chopped garlic
- 6 sprigs fresh thyme
- Salt and freshly ground pepper

Preheat the oven to 400 degrees, with a rack in the middle.

Core the tomatoes and cut them in half horizontally. Coat the bottom of a shallow roasting pan or rimmed baking sheet with ¼ cup of the oil. Sprinkle the garlic over the oil, then scatter the thyme sprigs over the garlic. Season the cut sides of the tomatoes with salt and pepper and place them cut side down on the garlic and thyme. Drizzle the remaining ¼ cup oil over the tomatoes. Roast for 30 minutes, or until the skins have blistered and the tomatoes are soft.

Remove the pan from the oven and let the tomatoes cool until they can be handled. Then pull off and discard the blistered skin. Discard the thyme sprigs. Transfer the juices remaining in the pan to a small saucepan, scraping everything off the bottom of the roasting pan. Add the skinned tomatoes and simmer for 10 to 12 minutes, mashing the tomatoes against the side of the pan with a wooden spoon until you have a coarse-textured puree. Taste, and add more salt and pepper if desired. Keep warm.

St. Paul (Shrimp Egg Foo Yong)

ST. LOUIS, MISSOURI

St. Louis is a city of weird culinary specialties. It is home of sauced pig snoots (in barbecue parlors), fried brain sandwiches (in taverns), toasted ravioli (which is actually deep-fried), chili mac à la mode (with a fried egg on top), and the amazing chili and potato omelet known as a slinger or, at the Goody Goody Diner, a Wilbur. Strangest of all St. Louis signature dishes is the St. Paul, a sandwich sold only in cheap chop suey parlors—of which the city has plenty.

We asked local historians, owners of Chinese restaurants, and city food critics, and none had a clue as to where the St. Paul came from and how it got its name, nor was anybody willing to go on record with a recipe. We would guess the inspiration was either Saint Paul the saint or St. Paul the city in Minnesota, but neither of those explanations gives a clue about the oddball sandwich's provenance. Who knows?

What matters is that it's a taste treat in a cheap-eats sort of way: a patty of egg foo yong (*sans* gravy) served on white bread, dressed with pickles and a slice of onion (and, optionally, American cheese). Like egg foo yong, St. Pauls come in various flavors: pork, ham, chicken, beef, or shrimp. This is a recipe we developed several years ago after returning from a St. Paul–eating expedition and watching several different cooks prepare it.

2 large eggs
½ cup bean sprouts
1 tablespoon minced scallion, white part only
1 tablespoon minced mushroom
1 water chestnut, diced
3 medium shrimp, peeled and diced
1 tablespoon peanut oil
  Salt and freshly ground pepper
4 slices soft white bread
2 slices American cheese (optional)

Beat the eggs in a small bowl. Add the sprouts, scallion, mushroom, water chestnut, and shrimp.

Heat the peanut oil in a small skillet. Pour in the egg mixture and fry, turning it once, until light brown, 1 to 2 minutes. When it is browned on both sides, remove the patty from the skillet and quickly drain it on a paper towel. Season to taste with salt and pepper. Cut the egg patty in half, place each half on a slice of white bread, top with the cheese if desired, place the remaining slices of bread on top, and serve.

Tuna Experience

One of our most fondly remembered sandwich shops is the Hoagie Experience, which had two or three outlets in Philadelphia. The dining room was done up in a screaming chartreuse so bright you needed sunglasses. Signs were everywhere, some listing the various combination sandwiches available, others referring to your progress as you worked your way from the order window—"This is the beginning of your experience" to "This is the end of your experience" (above the trash cans).

The variety of sandwiches available was nearly infinite, ranging from lo-cal turkey to the design-it-yourself Great Experience of any six meats and two cheeses a customer desired. The hoagies (aka heroes, grinders, submarines, zeps, spukkies) were delightful, and we grew especially enamored of one called the Tuna Experience, which, when toasted in the oven, becomes an Italian-accented tuna melt.

MAKES 2 LARGE SANDWICHES

1	7-ounce can albacore tuna, drained and flaked
⅓	cup minced celery
2	tablespoons chopped sweet pickle
1	teaspoon minced onion
⅓–½	cup mayonnaise
1	teaspoon Dijon mustard
½	teaspoon fresh lemon juice
2	8- to 10-inch lengths French or Italian bread
2–3	tablespoons olive oil
6	slices provolone cheese, at room temperature
	Shredded lettuce
6–8	slices tomato

Combine the tuna, celery, pickle, onion, mayonnaise, mustard, and lemon juice in a medium bowl. Blend well but do not pulverize.

Slice the bread in half horizontally, and if the loaves are thick, scoop out some of the inside to create a hollow to hold the ingredients. Drizzle the olive oil along the inside of the pieces. Pile in the tuna salad and top with the cheese, then the lettuce and tomato, and close the sandwiches.

If desired, the sandwiches can be toasted, whole, very briefly in a 350-degree oven, just long enough to crisp the bread. Serve.

✳ Walleye

TAVERN ON GRAND ✳ ST. PAUL, MINNESOTA

The sandwich forum at Roadfood.com was buzzing recently with a passionate discussion about a favorite sandwich made with Minnesota's state fish, the walleye. One partisan declared, "No bar or pub in Minnesota dare not have the walleye sandwich on its menu."

Walleye, a 2- to 4-pound game fish from the Great Lakes, also goes by the names walleye pike, pickerel, and, in France, *doré*. When quickly broiled or fried, its white flesh is moist, with a clean freshwater flavor. Northland taverns serve it deep-fried in a bun with mayo or tartar sauce, lettuce, and tomato. Beer on the side is vital.

For those who don't catch and cook their own, the best place to enjoy a classic Minnesota walleye sandwich is Tavern on Grand in St. Paul, which bills itself as "Minnesota's State Restaurant Serving Minnesota's State Fish." Decor is log-cabin rustic; there are twelve different beers on tap, and no matter where you sit in the bar, you have a good view of one of the many TVs positioned for everyone to watch whatever game is being broadcast. Here you can have a walleye basket (regular or Cajun-fried), walleye cakes, walleye shore lunch, walleye special (with a side of sirloin steak), blackened walleye, and a walleye sandwich with the fillets either broiled or deep-fried. The fried has a crust that is bliss to crunch and that also shores in more moist succulence. The following is our version of Tavern on Grand's sandwich, which one aficionado dubbed "the best dang walleye I ever ate."

4   5-ounce walleye fillets (pike and lake whitefish are possible substitutes)
2   large eggs, beaten
1   cup yellow cornmeal
½   teaspoon salt
¼   teaspoon freshly ground pepper
    Vegetable oil
4   6- to 8-inch-long hero rolls, sliced in half horizontally
    Butter for grilling the rolls (optional)
    Tartar sauce (page 39 or 51), Garlic Aïoli (page 197), or mayonnaise to taste
    Shredded iceberg lettuce
1   tomato, thinly sliced

Rinse the fillets and pat them dry. Put the beaten egg in a wide, shallow dish. Mix the cornmeal with the salt and pepper in another shallow dish. Dip the fillets in the egg and then dredge them in the cornmeal, coating them thoroughly.

In a cast-iron skillet, heat 1 inch of oil to 360 degrees (not quite smoking). Slip the fillets, two at a time, into the oil and cook for 4 to 5 minutes per side, or until they are dark gold and crisp. Remove from the pan with a slotted spoon and drain on paper towels.

Meanwhile, lightly toast the rolls or butter and grill them in a skillet. Spread them with tartar sauce, add lettuce and tomato, and finally the walleye fillets. Add the tops of the rolls, cut each sandwich in half, and serve immediately.

Whitefish Salad

WOLFIE COHEN'S RASCAL HOUSE ✳ MIAMI BEACH, FLORIDA

Near the entrance to the Rascal House, where those standing in line can ponder it, is this Damon Runyon quote: "As I see it, there are two kinds of people in this world: people who love delis, and people you shouldn't associate with." Opened in 1954, the same year as the grandiose Fontainebleau Hotel at the other end of the beach, the Rascal House is a world-class delicatessen with a gigantic menu of comfort-food soup, schmaltzy chopped liver, crisp potato pancakes, hot plates, mile-high sandwiches, and classic New York egg creams. Meals begin with puckery pickles dished out in stainless steel bowls: sours, half-sours, dills, pickled tomatoes and/or pickled cabbage. The coleslaw is strong and bracing, and if you are eating something other than a sandwich, you get a basket full of onion rolls, dinner rolls, sour-crusted rolls, salt-spangled rye bread, and pumpernickel rolls. Service is provided by an appropriately brusque staff of white-uniformed waitresses, each of whom is outfitted with an effulgent personalized hankie pinned to her left shoulder.

Among the true deli attractions is the whitefish salad. While you can enjoy it as knife-and-fork fodder on a plate with garnishes, it's best sandwiched between slices of rye or on a fresh bulkie roll.

WHITEFISH SALAD

1	2-pound smoked whitefish, skinned and boned, or 2 pounds smoked trout fillets
2	celery stalks, diced
2	tablespoons finely chopped red onion
1	cup sour cream
2	tablespoons mayonnaise
2	teaspoons fresh lemon juice
2	tablespoons minced fresh dill
4-6	slices rye bread or 4-6 bulkie rolls
4	tablespoons (½ stick) butter

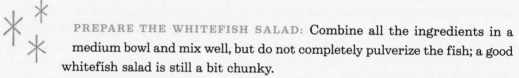

PREPARE THE WHITEFISH SALAD: Combine all the ingredients in a medium bowl and mix well, but do not completely pulverize the fish; a good whitefish salad is still a bit chunky.

ASSEMBLE THE SANDWICHES: Spread the bread slices with the butter. Then add the whitefish salad to the bottom slices, cap with the top slices, and serve.

Will Special (Italian Dagwood)

RIVIERA ITALIAN IMPORTED FOODS ✳ CHICAGO, ILLINOIS

"Da Riv," as Chicagoans know Riviera Italian Imported Foods, is not a restaurant. It is a grocery store where people come to buy house-made marinara, giardiniera, and arancini (fried rice balls), as well as imported olives and olive oil, meats, and cheeses. Around lunchtime, one or more members of the Pugliese family stake out the deli counter and make sandwiches for neighborhood folk and pilgrims who know this modest shop for its unique Italian submarine.

Sandwiches are wrapped to go or presented in flimsy cardboard boats, and sometimes a table is set up on the sidewalk, where you can sit down and dine to the tune of traffic on Harlem Avenue. When the weather's inclement, though, you are on your own.

The aroma of meats and cheeses here is delirious, and the choices are staggering. The menu lists three kinds of mortadella and five variations of prosciutto—smoked, domestic, from Parma, cotto (cooked with spices), and a prosciutto salami. Any and all are available in a sandwich, for which you choose your own fresh-baked Italian roll from a basket near the counter. Hand the bread to the sandwich man and tell him what you want.

The menu above the counter has no listing for the Will Special, but that is the go-to sandwich for those in the know—a dagwood of meats and cheese created by and named for a customer who is a regular contributor to the wonderful Chicago food Web site lthforum.com, who described his moment of creation as the result of "a particular fit of gluttony."

When gathering meats for this sandwich, ask the counterman to slice everything very, very thin. Although hefty, the Will Special should be an elegant sandwich.

3   slices hot sopressata
3   slices hot capicola
3   slices prosciutto cotto
4   slices prosciutto
1   large roll or 6- to 8-inch length Italian bread, sliced in half horizontally
4   slices fresh mozzarella cheese
Optional condiments: 2 tablespoons Giardiniera (recipe follows) or roasted red peppers (page 89)
Olive oil and freshly ground pepper if not using Giardiniera or peppers

Fold the meats onto the bottom half of the roll. Arrange the mozzarella on the meat and then cover it with the giardiniera or peppers or spritz the underside of the top of the roll with olive oil and sprinkle it with pepper. Close the sandwich and serve.

*⁎⁎ Giardiniera

MAKES 1 CUP

3 celery stalks, minced

1 small garlic clove, minced

½ red bell pepper, seeded and minced

1 plum tomato, finely chopped

2 tablespoons small capers with 1 tablespoon caper juice

½ teaspoon crushed red pepper flakes

1 teaspoon dried oregano

⅓ cup olive oil

2 tablespoons fresh lemon juice

Combine all the ingredients in a bowl and toss to mix. Cover and let the mixture steep at room temperature for at least 24 hours, preferably 48, tossing a few times each day.

Yaquina Oysters

DAN & LOUIS OYSTER BAR ✳ PORTLAND, OREGON

Founded in the early 1900s by Louis Wachsmuth, whose father's shipwreck in Yaquina Bay led to the discovery of the unique oysters that grow there, Dan & Louis is one of the oldest fish houses in Portland—and one of the most handsome. Its varnished wood walls are as plush as a yacht's, and it is bedecked floor to ceiling with an accumulation of nautical bibelots and historical pictures, documents, and maps that tell of Portland since Louis started serving food here.

Yaquina Bay oysters are small but not petite; they are meaty and have a bright, quietly briny flavor. Delicious in Dan & Louis's signature oyster stew, easy to eat on the half-shell, available also as one-shot oyster shooters or a whole oyster cocktail, Yaquinas were once almost extinct because so many of them were sent down to San Francisco's fancy restaurants. Now the delicious little mollusks thrive in Yaquina Bay.

One of the best things to do with them is to pan-fry them. That demands a delicate touch, because any sort of thick dough or breading will overwhelm the oysters' fragile flavor, but if it is done right, as it is for Dan & Louis's Yaquina sandwich, the result is ocean succulence incarnate.

If Yaquina oysters are not available to you (and they likely won't be if you aren't in the Pacific Northwest), this recipe works fine with any small to mid-size oyster with a not-too-assertive flavor. (Pacific Northwest oysters are available via next-day delivery, and at an accordingly high price, from the Lighthouse Deli & Fish Company in South Beach, Oregon: www.lighthousedeli.com.)

MAKES 2 SANDWICHES

1	teaspoon salt
1	cup cornmeal
18-20	freshly shucked Yaquina oysters (about 1 pint)
¼	cup clarified butter (page 152)
2	large rolls, or 4 slices sourdough bread
	Tartar sauce (optional; page 39 or 51)

Stir the salt into the cornmeal in a wide, shallow dish. Dredge the oysters in the cornmeal and let them sit for a few minutes on butcher paper or wax paper (not paper towels, which are too absorbent).

In a large, heavy skillet, heat the clarified butter to 360 degrees (not quite smoking). Slide the oysters into the skillet and cook, turning them once, for no more than 30 to 40 seconds per side. Immediately remove them from the oil with a slotted spoon and drain them on paper towels.

Serve in rolls or on sourdough bread, with tartar sauce if desired.

✱✱ Zep

NORRISTOWN, PENNSYLVANIA ✱✱

The logic of some names for stuffed big-loaf sandwiches is apparent. You are a hero if you eat one. It looks like a submarine. A lot of tooth work is required to devour a grinder. The term used around Norristown, Pennsylvania, northwest of Philadelphia (where hoagies rule), is zep, for which we've seen no conclusive explanation. We used to think zep was short for zeppelin, because the loaf in which it's made is shaped like one. But then a Pennsylvanian told us that zeps were named for *zeppoli,* which are balls of fried dough that are traditionally made by Sicilian cooks around Christmas. *Zeppoli* are best served hot and sprinkled liberally with powdered sugar, and aside from the fact that they're made of dough, the connection between a zep and a *zeppole* still seems tenuous. We'll stick to our belief that it was named for the airship.

The difference between a zep and a hoagie isn't only a matter of name. Hoagies almost always are dressed with lettuce. A zep never is. Furthermore, while hoagies are made in a hundred different variations, with a whole world of cold cuts and cheeses and condiments at the sandwich maker's ready, a zep is made one and only one way. And it is served only in Norristown. The two top contenders for zep excellence in Norristown are Lou's and Eve's. At either, a half-size zep, which is a good 10 inches long and plenty of lunch for any healthy appetite, costs under $5.

The ingredients for making a zep at home are readily available except for a crucial element: the bread. All true zeps are made on rolls from Conshohocken Bakery in Conshohocken (79 Jones St., 610-825-9334). Assuming you can't get these loaves, be sure to use a muscular Italian bread with a leathery crust rather than a flaky one.

Norristown zeps traditionally are made with Dietz & Watson brand cotto salami. Cotto (cooked) salami is a semisoft cold cut that has the consistency of bologna but is dotted with pepper and garlic.

MAKES 1 SANDWICH

1	length muscular Italian bread, about 10 inches long
3	slices provolone cheese
6	slices cotto salami
3-4	slices tomato
3-4	thin slices sweet onion
½	teaspoon dried oregano
1	tablespoon olive oil
	Salt and freshly ground pepper
	Spritz of red wine vinegar (optional)

Slice the bread in half lengthwise and layer the provolone on the bottom half. Fold the salami and place it on the cheese so it fits the profile of the bread (do not cut the salami). Layer on the tomato and onion and scatter the oregano and olive oil on top. Season with salt and pepper to taste and sprinkle on a little vinegar if desired. Cap with the top half of the bread and serve.

Condiments

✳ Ketchup

MAKES 1 CUP

1	cup finely chopped sweet onion
1	6-ounce can tomato paste
¼	cup applesauce
⅓	cup cider vinegar
½–1	garlic clove, chopped
1	teaspoon salt
½	teaspoon freshly ground white pepper
¼	teaspoon ground cinnamon

Combine all the ingredients in a blender and blend until smooth. The ketchup will keep, covered and refrigerated, for about 1 week.

Mustard

- ¼ cup yellow mustard seeds
- 2-3 tablespoons dry mustard, depending on how hot you want it
- 1 teaspoon ground turmeric
- ⅔ cup water
- 4-5 tablespoons white vinegar
- 2-4 tablespoons dry white wine (optional)
- 2 tablespoons sugar
- 2 tablespoons olive oil
- 1 garlic clove, minced
- 1-2 teaspoons salt

Combine the mustard seeds, dry mustard, turmeric, and water in a medium saucepan and bring to a boil, stirring constantly. Remove from the heat, cover, and let stand at room temperature overnight.

Stir in 4 tablespoons vinegar, the wine (if using), sugar, olive oil, and garlic. Place over high heat, bring to a boil, and simmer for 5 minutes. Place in a food processor and blend until smooth. Taste, and add more ground mustard, vinegar, and/or salt to taste. Keep refrigerated. Well covered, it will keep for up to 2 weeks.

 # Mayonnaise

MAKES 1 CUP

2	large egg yolks, at room temperature
1	teaspoon sharp dry mustard
2	tablespoons fresh lemon juice
¼-½	teaspoon salt
¼	teaspoon freshly ground white pepper
1	cup extra-virgin olive oil
1	tablespoon white wine vinegar

Whisk the egg yolks in a small bowl until they thicken and have a smooth lemon yellow tint. Whisk in the mustard, 1 tablespoon of the lemon juice, salt, and pepper. Very gradually, a few drops at a time, whisk in ½ cup of the olive oil. Then add the remaining ½ cup very gradually, in the smallest stream possible, so the oil emulsifies and the mayonnaise does not curdle. Whisk in the remaining 1 tablespoon lemon juice and the vinegar.

Refrigerate. The mayonnaise will thicken as it cools. The mayonnaise will keep, covered and refrigerated, for up to 3 days.

Mail-Order Condiments

BOETJE'S STONE-GROUND DUTCH MUSTARD. Rich, grainy, and speckled with bits of mustard seeds, Boetje's has been a Midwest favorite since 1889.

877-726-3853
www.boetjefoods.com

EWEBERRY FARMS JAMS. Oregon is famous for delicious berries, and so it makes sense that some of the most vivid-flavored berry jams are sold by Eweberry Farms of Brownsville. Whether you are making a peanut butter sandwich or looking for a brilliant way to gild the fanciest multilayered teatime nibbles, we suggest dipping into a jar of Eweberry's cherry amaretto, marionberry, or blackberry apple jam.

541-466-3470
www.eweberry.com

KELCHNER'S HORSERADISH. Looking to make that beef sandwich buzz? Horseradish does the trick, especially if it is Kelchner's. Made in Bucks County, Pennsylvania, since 1938, this hot stuff is thick enough to spread easily onto meats with little of the drippiness evidenced by ordinary horseradish.

800-424-1952
www.pa-foods.com

MRS. ROWE'S APPLE BUTTER. There's nothing better on the side of an open-face hot turkey sandwich than a few tablespoons of Mrs. Rowe's molasses-dark apple butter. Mrs. Rowe is now gone, but her restaurant remains just off I-81 in Staunton, Virginia. You can also buy peach, whole cherry, blueberry, raspberry, and strawberry jellies.

540-886-1833
www.mrsrowes.com

WOEBER'S SUPREME MUSTARDS. Woeber's are the aristocracy of mustards. The company's Supreme line is extra-rich, extra-smooth, and extra-delicious. Varieties include Supreme Honey Mustard, Supreme Dijon, and Supreme Wasabi.

800-548-2929
www.woebermustard.com

Index